Discovering
LONDON CURIOSITIES

John Wittich

Shire Publications Ltd

CONTENTS

The cover illustration is 'A New Love Song Only Ha'penny a Piece', one of the 'Cries of London' painted by F. Wheatley RA.

 First published 1973. Second edition 1980. Third edition 1990. Number 165 in the Discovering series. ISBN 0 7478 0074 X.

Printed in Great Britain by C. I. Thomas & Sons (Haverfordwest) Ltd, Press Buildings, Merlins Bridge, Haverfordwest, Dyfed SA61 1XE.

1. THE ROYAL PARKS TO NELSON

The curiosities mentioned in chapters 1-4 may be visited in the order described by reference to the maps.

Collectively **Hyde Park** and **Kensington Gardens** cover an area of 636 acres, the former royal hunting park of Henry VIII accounting for 361 acres and its neighbour, Kensington Gardens, about 275 acres. It is difficult to distinguish their boundaries but the contents are quite different: Hyde Park has acre after acre of pleasant green 'fields' while Kensington Gardens boast flower beds, a boating pond, and well defined avenues of trees leading towards Kensington Palace. Originally the property of Westminster Abbey, it became Crown property at the dissolution of the abbey in 1536. Elizabeth I held military reviews in the park, and it was first opened to the public in the reign of James I, and later in the same century horse and foot races were held in it. After the triumph of the Roundheads all the royal parks were sold to speculators but they were reopened to the public at the restoration of the monarchy in 1660. Hurling matches, a combination of present-day football and all-in wrestling, were also played in the park. Samuel Pepys records in his diary coming 'finely dressed' to the parks and taking part in what has been described as a fashion parade in order to be noticed by King Charles II.

When William III ascended the throne in 1689 he bought the house of the second Earl of Nottingham which was built on the edge of Hyde Park. Nottingham House, as it was then called, became Kensington Palace and about twenty-six acres of Hyde Park became Kensington Gardens. Queen Caroline, the wife of George II, added another 200 acres, and Queen Victoria transferred the portion of Hyde Park around the **Albert Memorial** (1) to the gardens.

Once described as an overgrown medieval reliquary, the **Albert Memorial** (1) contains a seated figure of Prince Albert, the Prince Consort, husband of Queen Victoria; lying open on his knees is the catalogue of the Great Exhibition of 1851. Round the base of the memorial are some 170 figures depicting the arts, and the four continents are shown in groups at the foot of the steps. The cross on the top was a victim of the Second World War, but afterwards was replaced —the wrong way round!

The ceremonial gates (2) which Queen Victoria unlocked when she officially opened the Great Exhibition now mark the boundary between Hyde Park and Kensington Gardens.

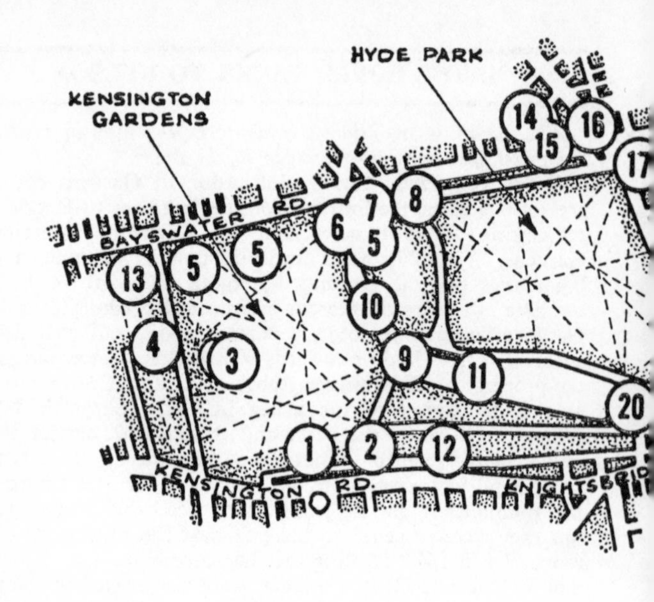

0 220 440 660 880

YARDS

ROYAL PARKS TO NELSON

1. Albert Memorial
2. Ceremonial gates
3. Round Pond
4. Sunken garden
5. Paddington boundary stones
6. River Westbourne
7. Queen Anne's summer-house
8. Victoria Gate
9. Serpentine bridge
10. Long Water
11. Serpentine
12. Site of Crystal Palace
13. Broad Walk
14. St George's graveyard
15. Tyburn Convent
16. Site of Tyburn Tree
17. Marble Arch
18. Achilles statue
19. Apsley House
20. The Dell
21. Royal Artillery Memorial
22. Wellington memorial arch
23. Porter's rest
24. Constitution Hill
25. Green Park
26. Queen Victoria Memorial
27. Royal Mews
28. Flood-water spout
29. The Mall
30. St James's Park lake
31. Berry Brothers and Rudd, Lock's
32. Pickering Place
33. Birdcage Walk
34. 'Bloody Mary' statue
35. Duck Island
36. The Citadel
37. Duke of York's Column
38. Waterloo Place
39. Statue of Charles I
40. Harrington House
41. Nelson's Column
42. Imperial standards
43. National Gallery
44. St Martin's in the Fields

Although it is always known as **The Round Pond** (3), from the air its shape is like the outline of a Tudor rose. Here boys of all ages come and sail their boats, and it is recorded that Shelley, the poet, sailed paper boats on the pond, sometimes making them from banknotes!

Laid out by 'Dutch' William and Queen Mary, as a formal sunken garden (4) and first opened to the public in 1909, the floral displays form a pleasant oasis; surrounded, cloister-like, by a lime tree walk, the garden is a reminder of the formal gardens of the eighteenth century. At several places in the north portion of Kensington Gardens are the boundary stones (5) of the former Paddington Parish (PP) and the old Metropolitan Borough of Paddington (MBP), but why Paddington should penetrate into the gardens is apparently not known.

Although today most of the **river Westbourne** is underground it can be seen trickling down towards the Serpentine behind the former pump-house (6). The river starts its journey in Hampstead, passes through Hyde Park (through the Serpentine Lake) and flows into the river Thames by Ranelagh Gardens. Between here and Chelsea it also passes *over* the underground railway at Sloane Square where the pipe can be seen today.

Prior to the opening of Kensington Gardens to the public (originally on Saturdays only, and provided full dress was worn) the area was part of the private gardens of Kensington Palace. In the early eighteenth century Sir Christopher Wren designed a summer-house for the personal use of Queen Anne (7), in order that she might enjoy the pleasures of the gardens. Today it serves as a resting place for members of the public.

In 1880 the Duchess of Cambridge received permission to bury her favourite dog by **Victoria Gate** (8) in Hyde Park. Today there are over eight hundred little tombstones in memory of dogs, cats and birds, some well worth reading. The key is available from the park's police station.

Dividing the **'Serpentine'** (11) from **'The Long Water'** (10) in Hyde Park is the only remaining bridge in London designed by Rennie, built in 1828 (9). It is an excellent vantage point from which to view London's changing skyline. The park was formerly watered by the river Westbourne, but as this only formed itself into a number of unsightly ponds the 'Long Water' or 'Serpentine' was formed in 1730. Any extra water required to keep the standard level is supplied from a pump on Duck Island, St James's Park. In 1816 Shelley's first wife, Harriet Westbrook, committed suicide by drowning herself in the Serpentine; her body was buried, presumably in unconsecrated ground, in St Mary's churchyard, Paddington Green, the entry in the burial register reading 'unknown person drowned in Serpentine'.

One of the greatest occasions that Hyde Park has ever seen was when the Great Exhibition was held here in 1851. The vast glasshouse, designed by Joseph Paxton, soon became known as the Crystal Palace, and after the exhibition was over the building was re-erected at Sydenham in south London, where it was destroyed by fire in 1936. The site chosen (12) occupied an area 1,843 feet by 450 feet, at one end of which were two elm trees, and controversy arose as to whether they should be cut down or not. However, Paxton redesigned that part of the giant glasshouse to accommodate them, and their stumps can still be seen today. The exhibition, in which exhibitors from all countries showed their industrial and artistic skills, was a brilliant success, and made a profit which was used for the setting up of some of London's great museums.

Originally planted in the time of George II and Queen Caroline, **Broad Walk** (13) is now only a shadow of its former self, the original trees having been replaced in 1953 because of disease. There is a legend that the trees were arranged in the same position as the Brigade of Guards at the Battle of Blenheim.

On one side of Broad Walk, at the entrance to the **Children's Playground** (13) in the Gardens, stands the **Elfin Oak**, which originally grew in Richmond Park; the 'little people' on the oak were carved by Ivor Innes, and from the natural forms of crosses, holes and indentations the artist has created a world of fairies, elves and pixies to the delight of children of all ages. The playground itself was provided by James Barrie, the author of *Peter Pan,* who prior to the opening of the gardens to the general public, had his own private entrance and key to the grounds. He lived in a house almost opposite in the Bayswater Road.

On land once owned by the Bishop of London in the Bayswater Road was, until 1970, the burial ground of **St George's, Hanover Square** (14). Created in 1763, and covering one acre, it was used until it became full in 1852. Later it was used as a garden and the Royal Toxophilitic Society set up its butts in a cleared portion. Lawrence Sterne, author of *Tristram Shandy* and *A Sentimental Journey,* was buried here in 1768; apparently after his burial body-snatchers removed his corpse from its grave and sold it to the Professor of Anatomy at Cambridge, who on seeing his late friend's body on the slab returned it post-haste to London. The artist, Paul Sandby, who died in 1809, was also buried here. Born in 1721 at Nottingham, he is reputed to have introduced the aquatint into England from France; certainly he and his brother Thomas used this technique. Paul produced a series of etchings of Hyde Park and a number of his prints are in the Royal Library at Windsor where his brother was Deputy Ranger of Windsor Forest. In order to prevent any further body-snatching from the graveyard two six-foot walls, three feet apart, were erected. Apparently it is not possible to throw a corpse up and over such a wall! The site is now occupied by flats.

Beside the **Tyburn Convent** (15) is the smallest house in London. Only three feet six inches wide, it was built to block a passage which the owner wanted to make private.

On a triangular road island opposite the Odeon Theatre, Edgware Road, is a plaque commemorating the site of **Tyburn Tree** (16). The tree, last used in 1783 for the hanging of John Austin, stood twelve feet high, was triangular in shape and was capable of hanging eight people on each of its three sides. It was not unusual for gallows and other places of execution to be sited at the entrance to towns as a warning to potential criminals. This tree was the end of the road for felons from Newgate Prison.

A 'Tyburn Ticket', a much sought-after certificate exempting the holder from any parish or ward offices, was granted for successful prosecutions in criminal actions which terminated in capital punishment. The selling of the ticket was permitted only once, the highest known amount paid for one being £280 in 1818. The act granting Tyburn Tickets was entered on the statute book in William III's reign (1689-1702) and repealed in 1818.

Standing now at the important road junction of Bayswater Road, Edgware Road, Oxford Street and Park Lane, it must be difficult to remember that the **Marble Arch** (17) once formed the entrance gateway to Buckingham Palace. Designed by the favourite architect of George IV, John Nash, who based it on the famous Arch of Constantine in Rome, it is built of Carrara marble and cost £100,000 (the central gates over £3,000), and Chantry's equestrian statue of George IV, now in Trafalgar Square, which cost over £9,000, should have been placed on top. Marble Arch was moved to its present site in 1851—because, it is said, the royal coaches could not conveniently pass through! It is also a memorial to Lord Nelson and contains one of the smallest police stations in London.

Just behind Apsley House (Wellington Museum) stands the memorial of the Ladies of England to the first Duke of Wellington. Usually known as the **Achilles statue** (18) it is, in fact, Westmacott's version of the horse-tamers on the Quirinal in Rome and was cast from cannons captured by Wellington's armies at Salamanca, Vittoria and Waterloo. When it was erected in 1822 a correspondent of the *Morning Herald* wrote complaining about the nudity: 'If my mother had caught any of her children looking at such an object she would have soundly whipped them'. In 1889 Friese-Greene took the first recorded moving pictures, of his cousin with his son, in this vicinity.

A grateful Queen Anne gave to her victorious general, the

Duke of Marlborough, Blenheim Palace in Oxfordshire. But the grateful King William IV gave to his victorious soldier, the first Duke of Wellington, the building we now know as **Apsley House** (19). Today it is the Wellington Museum where you may see the Waterloo Gallery, the setting for the Waterloo Dinner between the years 1816 and 1829 (now held at Windsor Castle). Wellington's opponent, Napoleon of France, was a short man, but here you can see Canova's nude statue which is more than life-size. Napoleon, it is said, disliked the statue.

Standing in **The Dell** (20) is a long stone which, according to legend, Charles I brought from Stonehenge in Wiltshire. In fact it is a piece of Cornish granite weighing over seven tons which, in 1861, formed part of a drinking fountain that was subsequently removed.

Designed by C. S. Jaeger and unveiled in the 1920s, the **Royal Artillery Memorial** (21) at Hyde Park Corner represents a howitzer of the First World War. The gun is so angled that if a shell were fired with sufficient propulsion, it would land in the middle of the Somme battlefield in France, where so many Gunners were killed in 1916.

Inside the **Arch** (22) at the head of Constitution Hill is a police station. The arch itself, designed by Decimus Burton, is a memorial to the Duke of Wellington whose equestrian statue (now on a parade ground in Aldershot) once adorned the arch. The figures on top of the arch today are known as the Quadriga and it is said that the sculptor, Captain Adrian Jones, and a few of his friends had been *inside* the group before it was finally completed.

A reminder of the days when men earned their living by carrying heavy loads on their backs can be seen at the Hyde Park Corner end of Piccadilly (23)—it is a **Porter's Rest:** here a porter could rest his load, still strapped to his back, before continuing his journey.

A number of unsuccessful attempts to assassinate Queen Victoria took place in **Constitution Hill** (24). Here, too, Sir Robert Peel, founder of the Metropolitan Police Force, was thrown from his horse in 1850.

In 1767 George III, wishing to enlarge the grounds of Buckingham Palace, 'acquired' a few acres from Little St James's Park, known today as **Green Park** (25). In the north-west corner was a reservoir belonging to the Chelsea Waterworks which held 1.5 million gallons of water, at a height of forty-four feet above the high-water mark of the Thames;

from the reservoir it was possible to view the hills of Wimbledon, and the Crystal Palace at Sydenham. It is said that as the park is on the banks of the river Tyburn it is hardly surprising that there are no flower beds, while another story as to why no flowers would ever grow in the park was that Henry VIII, wishing to use the nearby St James's Hospice for a banquet, turned the nuns out into the ice and snow for the night; many of the sisters died, and as a result 'no flowers will ever grow in the park'. To celebrate the peace of 1814 a vast Temple of Concord was erected, which together with illuminations, paintings and fireworks must have presented a joyful sight for the Londoner.

The **Queen Victoria Memorial** (26), designed by Sir Aston Webb, who later re-fronted Buckingham Palace, stands in solitary glory at the Palace end of The Mall. Built of white marble and weighing 2,300 tons it stands 82 feet high with a seated statue of the Queen on its east side, the other three sides being occupied by statues of Charity (west), Truth (north) and Justice (south), and the whole being surrounded by bronze groups representing Progress, Peace, Manufacture, Agriculture, Painting, Architecture and Shipbuilding. The sculptor, Sir Thomas Brock, shows the Queen wearing her wedding ring on her right hand in deference to her husband's continental origin.

Behind **Buckingham Palace,** the London home of the Queen, are the **Royal Mews** (27), which is open to members of the public on Wednesday and Thursday afternoons for a small fee. Here can be seen the Coronation Coach, used only on the coronation day of the kings and queens of Britain, the Irish State Coach which is used annually for the State Opening of Parliament and numerous other horse-drawn coaches used by members of the royal family. In addition, there are a number of motor-cars, and, of course, the horses and stables of the royal household.

The lake in **St James's Park** (30) is fed by the waters of the river Tyburn which today is one of London's lost rivers, now channelled underground and serving as a flood-relief pipe. After heavy rainstorms water can be seen pouring from a spout in the waterhead (28).

Before the reconstruction of the area as part of the national memorial to Queen Victoria, a small kiosk at the end of **The Mall** (29) sold milk straight from the cow. The old line of the road is now used as a riding track at the side of the new road; the original avenue was laid out in the seventeenth century at the instigation of Charles II. Described as the finest processional way in Europe it makes an excellent route for state processions.

St James's Park was first formed in the reign of Henry VIII (1509-1547) and walled in as a deer park. Elizabeth I (1558-1603) held fetes and tourneys there, while James I (1603-1625) had an open menagerie which included everything from hawks to elephants. Charles I (1625-1649) took his last walk on earth through the park on his way to execution at Whitehall. After his return from exile at the French court Charles II (1660-1685) asked Le Notre, the famous French landscape architect responsible for the Tuileries and Versailles gardens, to design a layout for the park, but Le Notre, it is said, refused to disturb a place of such natural beauty. Charles II contented himself by turning the swamps and ponds into a canal which was later made into the lake by John Nash (1752-1835).

The lake of the park (30). contains a wide variety of birds and fish but is only four feet deep. In winter, provided the ice is thick enough, ice-skating is permitted on the lake. During the First World War the lake was drained and office huts erected in the space.

Sometime in the eighteenth century members of the aristocracy living in this part of London discovered that The Coffee Mill, the former name of Berry Brothers and Rudd, at 3 St James's Street (31), had a pair of scales used to weigh the bulk coffee supplies, and that these were large enough to weigh a person. Over the years many famous and infamous personages have used these scales, including the late Aga Khan, who gave his weight in gold for charitable purposes, the late Duke of Windsor, and Prince Louis Napoleon (Napoleon III). A reminder of the early days of Berry Brothers is the eighteenth-century shop sign with its coffee mill; the shops are virtually unaltered since they were built in about 1730, and contain an interesting collection of rare old wine bottles, another reminder of the company's connection with the grocery and wine trades.

Lock's, London's oldest hatters, can be found at **6 St James's Street** (31). Their window display is a veritable museum of old hats, some being older than the firm itself, which was founded in 1793. An early customer of the shop was Mr William Coke who asked that a hat be designed for him to wear when out hunting; when it was ready he tried it on but was dissatisfied and, putting it on the floor, jumped on it—

the hat became known as the 'billycock' and was later developed into the bowler hat of today.

Passing through the archway at the side of Berry Brothers and Rudd, past a plaque on the alleyway's wall commemorating the office of the Republic of Texas, the inquisitive visitor will come to **Pickering Place** (32). Built in the eighteenth century for a Mr. William Pickering, it is an unspoilt Georgian backwater of London. The bust of Lord Palmerston in the courtyard reminds one that he lived here for a period of his life.

Birdcage Walk (33), which runs alongside St James's Park owes its name to the aviary owned by Charles II, which is said to have contained many exotic birds, including a crane with a wooden leg and a bird from the West Indies which took great delight in eating burning coals.

Tradition says that the statue of **Queen Anne** (34) was erected by the founder of the Bank of England, William Paterson, but there is no evidence for this, neither is the sculptor known. Once upon a time the children of the area used to invite the queen to come down, and when she declined they threw stones at her and called her 'Bloody Mary', confusing her with Queen Mary I. This incidence may have given rise to the story that every year, on the anniversary of her death, 1st August, she does come down from the pedestal but, not liking what she sees, returns before daybreak.

The three fountains were erected in the lake of St James's Park in order to aerate the water and to enable the fish to breathe more easily. At night floodlighting turns them into a wonderland of water and light. **Duck Island** (35) at the eastern end of the lake is a bird sanctuary.

The concrete building known as **The Citadel** on the corner of The Mall (36) is a large bunker-like construction built to house the war chiefs of the Second World War. It is now a listed building!

At the head of the steps which lead from The Mall to Waterloo Place stands the **Duke of York's column** (37); at the side there is a tree in a plot of ground, in which 'Giro', the favourite dog of the German Ambassador Hoescht, which died in 1934, is buried.

Whether they are left-over pieces of Carlton House or from the Duke of York's steps, the lumps of granite stone in **Waterloo Place** (38) form useful mounting blocks. The Duke of Wellington suggested that they be put to use for the benefit of the small man.

One of a number of crosses erected to commemorate where Edward I's first wife Eleanor's body rested on its way to burial in Westminster Abbey (though her heart was buried in the Blackfriars monastery in the City) stood where Charles I's statue now stands. It was from this memorial cross that distances to and from London were often measured, and a bronze plaque on the pavement commemorates this fact.

At the head of Whitehall and at the foot of Nelson's Column stands **Charles I's statue** (39), designed by Le Sueur. The horse's left front foot bears the date 1632, the year in which it was originally erected in King Street, near Covent Garden. During the Civil War it was hidden in the crypt of St Paul's Church, Covent Garden, and later sold to one Rivett who is said to have melted it down and sold the newly created pieces as souvenirs of the 'late King and Martyr'. But at the restoration of the monarchy in 1660 a miracle happened and it was found intact and given to Charles II who set it up on its present site.

The last remaining private mansion of Whitehall was **Harrington House** in Craig's Court (40). Built at the turn of the eighteenth century, today it houses the Whitehall Telephone Exchange offices.

Trafalgar Square and **Nelson's Column** (41) are all part of a scheme of 1829 to commemorate Horatio, Lord Nelson (1758-1805), the column being erected between 1840 and 1843. The 185-foot column is made of Devon granite, culminating in a bronze capital, and is the work of W. Railton (1801-1877); the 18-foot high statue of Nelson is by E. H. Bailey (1788-1867), and the guardians of the column, four lions by Sir Edwin Landseer (1802-1873), were placed here in 1868. Around the base on the west side a number of the stones are badly chipped and this has been pointed out as war damage—and so it is in a way. For while celebrating the Armistice of 1918 some members of the armed forces accidentally set light to a workman's hut. The fire was so great that the heat split several of the stones—hence the damage. A move to repair them after the Second World War was rejected. The square was designed by Sir Charles Barry (1795-1860) and the fountains were redesigned in 1939 by Sir Edwin Lutyens (1869-1944).

On the north side of Trafalgar Square, between the busts of Admirals Jellicoe and Cunningham, are the **Imperial Standards**, put there under the Act of 1876 (42); they show how long an inch, foot, yard, rod, pole or perch should be under the Law. The dictionary definition of an inch is that it is one-twelfth of an English or American foot. However, originally it was 'three standard ears of corn placed end to end'.

When Carlton House was demolished in 1827 much of the stone was used elsewhere, including the portico of the **National Gallery** (43) in Trafalgar Square. Visitors to the Gallery should also look at the mosaics on the floor where such famous persons as Greta Garbo, T. S. Eliot and Sir Winston Churchill can be seen.

Built to the design of James Gibbs (1682-1754), who had intended to build a round church, **St Martin's in the Fields** (44) was completed in 1726. It is the only church in London to have a Royal Pew, although there seems to be no evidence that it has ever been used, in spite of the fact that St Martin's is the parish church of Buckingham Palace, St James's Palace and Marlborough House. The date of the church, together with the architect's name, can be found on the portico of the building. George I (1714-1727) donated £29,000 towards the building fund, and, in gratitude the people made him churchwarden—a post he did not wish to hold! Until recently one could not resign from the post of churchwarden; nonetheless at a subsequent meeting of the church council, George's resignation was accepted, but he was fined £1,000 which, doubtless, went to swell the coffers of the building fund. Nell Gwyn (1650-1687), actress and mistress of Charles II, was buried in the previous church; at her funeral Thomas Tenison, Archbishop of Canterbury from 1695 to 1715, preached. While vicar of St Martin's, Tenison founded a school for boys which later in its history was to occupy Hogarth's house in Leicester Square. Today the school occupies a site opposite the Oval Cricket Ground on land owned by the Duchy of Cornwall.

2. ALONG THE RIVER THAMES

Founded in 1673 by the Society of Apothecaries of London, the **Chelsea Physic Gardens** (1) continues today its research work in the botanical field. The gardens are open to the public on Wednesday and Sunday afternoons from April to October. Sir Hans Sloane bought the freehold and gave it to the society on condition that they would keep it 'for the manifestation of the glory, power and wisdom of God.' In 1732 cotton seeds from these gardens were sent to America, beginning the great cotton industry of that country.

On the site of a former monastic almshouse, theological college and military internment camp stands the **Royal Chelsea Hospital** (2), founded by Charles II (1660-1685), at the instigation of Nell Gwyn as a place of retirement for old soldiers, with financial help from William Sancroft, Archbishop of Canterbury from 1678 to 1691, who gave £1,000. The architect responsible for the design of the building was Christopher Wren (1632-1723). The hospital has accommodation for four hundred veterans and is open to the public daily. In the Great Hall, the refectory of the Hospital, the Duke of Wellington lay in state until his burial in St Paul's Cathedral, and a drawing in the hall shows the elaborate catafalque. Charles II's statue by Grinling Gibbons, in the Figure or Centre Court, is decked with oak leaves on Founder's Day, 29th May, his birthday, to commemorate his escape after the battle of Worcester in 1651, when he hid in an oak tree.

Ranelagh Gardens (3), once one of the most popular pleasure gardens in London, today form part of the grounds of the Royal Hospital. The gardens came into being when the estates of the Earl of Ranelagh were sold and bought by speculators. The famous Rotunda, opened in April 1742, was a great success with musical performances from early morning throughout the day. But early in the nineteenth century the public grew tired of the gardens and they were finally closed in 1805.

From the river, or from the opposite bank, can be seen the embankment aperture (4) through which the **river Westbourne** flows into the Thames.

Battersea Park (5) covers nearly 200 acres and was laid out in the mid nineteenth century by Sir James Pennethorne. It is recorded that asparagus was first cultivated in England here before the existence of the park. Because of the solitude of the area duels were often fought here, one of the last being between the Duke of Wellington and Lord Winchelsea.

Victoria Station stands on piles over the basin of the former **Grosvenor Canal,** one of the many eighteenth-century inlets into the banks of the river. Much of the canal has been filled in today. However, the entrance (6) is still in use and Westminster City Council use part of the site for their Cleansing Department's works.

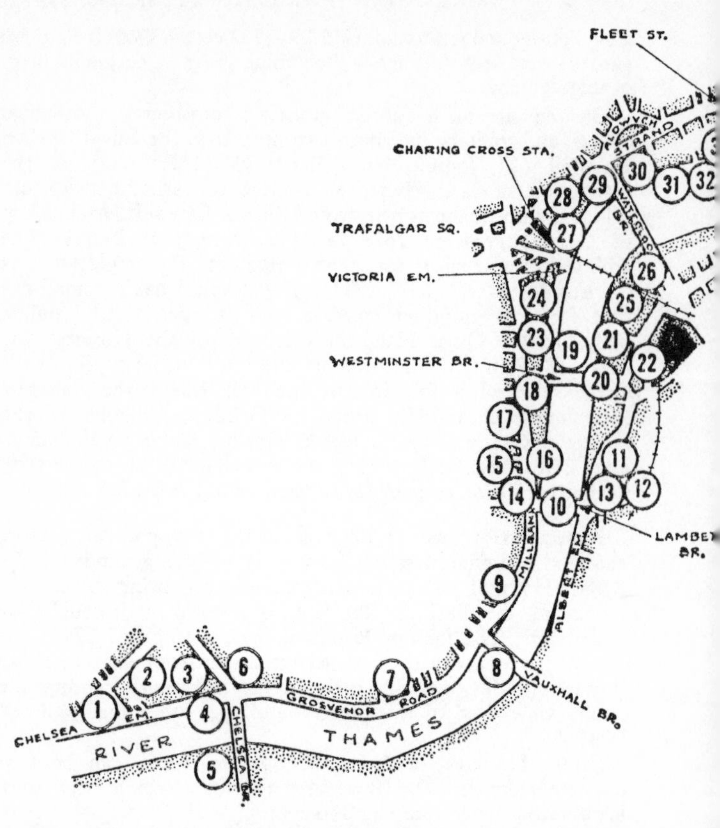

Containing over one thousand flats, **Dolphin Square** (7) is one of the largest self-contained blocks of its kind in Europe, and is named after a nearby 'dolphin' pump used for drawing water from the river. At one time the Royal Army Clothing Department stood on this site.

The first bridge to connect Vauxhall on the south side of the Thames and Pimlico on the north was built between 1811 and 1815. This was replaced by the present **Vauxhall Bridge** (8) in 1906. Note in particular the larger-than-life figures on the riverside; these include Architecture holding in her hands a miniature of St Paul's Cathedral. This was the first bridge in London to carry trams over the river.

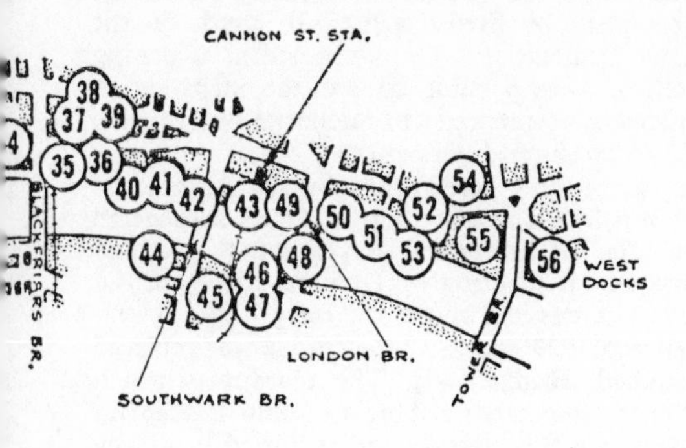

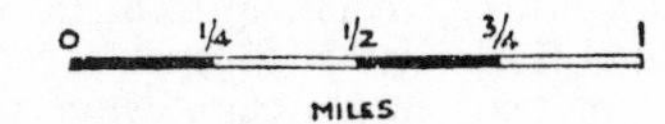

ALONG THE RIVER THAMES

1. Chelsea Physic Gardens
2. Royal Chelsea Hospital
3. Ranelagh Gardens
4. River Westbourne
5. Battersea Park
6. Grosvenor Canal
7. Dolphin Square
8. Vauxhall Bridge
9. Tate Gallery
10. Lambeth Bridge
11. Lambeth Palace
12. St Mary's churchyard
13. St Mary's, Lambeth
14. ICI House
15. St John's, Smith Square
16. Victoria Tower Gardens
17. Jewel Tower
18. St Margaret's, Westminster
19. Boudicca's statue
20. Coade-stone lion
21. County Hall
22. General Lying-in Hospital
23. Scotland Yard
24. Ministry of Defence
25. Shell Building
26. Royal Festival Hall
27. York House Watergate
28. Carting Lane
29. Savoy Hill
30. Somerset House
31. Embankment
32. The 'Wellington'
33. City boundary
34. Sion College
35. Blackfriars Station
36. Mermaid Theatre
37. Printing House Square
38. Church Entry
39. Playhouse Yard
40. Baynard's Castle
41. Queenhithe
42. Vintners' Hall
43. Cannon Street Station
44. Wren's house
45. Globe Theatre site
46. Clink Street
47. Southwark Cathedral
48. London Bridge
49. Fishmongers' Hall
50. St Magnus the Martyr
51. Customs House
52. All Hallows Church
53. Tower Subway Kiosk
54. Tower Hill scaffold site
55. Tower of London
56. St Katherine's Docks

In the **Tate Gallery,** Millbank (9), are the nation's collections of paintings and sculpture by British artists. It stands on the site of the Millbank Penitentiary. Until the recent widening of the embankment it was possible to see the steps down which many prisoners, sentenced to deportation to the colonies, descended to be shipped abroad.

Originally there was a ferry here owned by the Archbishop of Canterbury whose palace is nearby, but in 1862 a suspension bridge replaced it. The Archbishop (John Sumner) received £2,200 in compensation. A painting by Leonard Knyff, in the Museum of London's possession, shows the ferry in the seventeenth century. Between 1929 and 1932 the bridge was replaced by the present **Lambeth Bridge** (10). The pineapples which form part of the decoration are a tribute to John Tradescant who introduced them into this country and is buried in nearby **St Mary's Churchyard** (12).

Although rarely open to members of the public **Lambeth Palace** (11) has much in it to interest any visitor to the buildings or grounds. The main gatehouse, built *c.* 1495, is the work of Cardinal Morton, Archbishop from 1485 to 1500, and is a rare example of Tudor work. Morton is perhaps best known as a collector of taxes in his capacity of Chancellor of the Exchequer. His method was simple and foolproof and it became known as 'Morton's Fork'. If on his visits round the country he was entertained in a royal manner, he made his host pay heavy taxes knowing that he could afford it, but if he visited a house where his methods of taxation were known, and consequently his host entertained him more sparingly, Morton maintained that this man must be saving his money and taxed him heavily as well. What he failed to get on one prong of his fork he got on the other!

Tradescant was the court gardener to Charles I and Henrietta Maria and a distinguished botanical traveller of the seventeenth century. His tomb in St Mary's Churchyard lies near Bligh's and shows crocodiles, a hydra (a multi-headed beast) and several buildings and ruins. On his death Tradescant's collections were taken over by Ashmole who later donated the entire collection to Oxford University, where it became the basis of the Ashmolean Museum.

Made of Coade Stone, the tomb of Vice-Admiral William Bligh—better known as Captain Bligh of the *Bounty*—stands to the east of the church. After the famous mutiny aboard his ship in 1787, Bligh and his eighteen loyal men were cast adrift and, after over 3,500 miles of adventurous journeyings, landed at Timor in the Dutch East Indies. Eleanor Coade (Sealey), the last of the stone-making family, is also buried here.

On 31st October 1972 the last service was held in **St Mary's, Lambeth Parish Church** (13), used for Christian worship for hundreds of years; the congregation then went in procession to the local Methodist church, whose premises they were to share. The tower, dating from 1377, is all that is left of the medieval church, the rest of the building being rebuilt by Philip Hardwick in fourteenth-century style in 1851. As it is so close to Lambeth Palace it is hardly surprising that several archbishops of Canterbury are buried here. The building was taken over by the Tradescant Trust, and is now the Museum of Garden History.

Imperial Chemical Industries House (14) and its neighbour **Thames House** were designed by Sir Frank Baines and built between 1929 and 1931. The doors of ICI House have no locks, being operated by electrical power; the bas-reliefs on them depict man from primitive to modern times.

Thanks to the Friends of **St. John's Church, Smith Square** (15) the church has now been superbly restored to its former glory after lying ruined for a number of years. Built in 1714-28 to the designs of Thomas Archer (1668-1743), it was one of the fifty churches planned by Act of Parliament in the early eighteenth century in and around London. When asked what type of church she would like to see here Queen Anne is alleged to have kicked over a footstool—hence the somewhat strange design of the building with its four corner towers pointing to the sky. Dickens in *Our Mutual Friend,* describes the church as being 'like a petrified monster, frightful and gigantic on its back with its legs in the air'. However, in order to build a platform over the marshy ground on which the church stands, the towers were required to support the weight of the building, and so prevent it from sinking into the ground. No longer used as a church, it is used for concerts and recitals.

In the **Victoria Tower Gardens** (16) stands a number of interesting memorials and statues among them the memorial to the abolitionists of slave trading in the British Empire, which originally stood in Parliament Square. Known as the Buxton Memorial Fountain it commemorates Thomas Buxton MP, the leader of the movement.

The exact origin of the **Jewel Tower** (17) is not known for certain, but Dean Stanley thought that it might have been used as a monastic prison at one time. Other authorities say that it was, as its name implies, the place where the Crown

Jewels were kept, possibly on the evening before coronations. However, it has been used as a depository for Parliamentary records by the Weights and Measures Department, and finally as an exhibition and display centre.

Although there were two earlier churches on the site, the present **St Margaret's Church, Westminster** (18), dates from the fifteenth century. The east window has an interesting and curious history: eventually, in 1758, the glass was placed in the church, but not before it had had a number of owners. Originally intended as a gift for Henry VII (1485-1509) on the betrothal of his son Prince Arthur (Henry VIII's elder brother) to Catherine of Aragon, the daughter of Ferdinand and Isabella of Spain, it arrived in this country after the deaths of both Henry VII and Arthur. The young prince kneels in the left-hand corner with St George of England as his nearside companion, and Catherine, with St Catherine of Sienna, is in the opposite corner. After his execution in 1618 the headless body of Sir Walter Raleigh was buried near the high altar.

Many poets and men of literature are buried in Poets Corner in **Westminster Abbey** and in the north-west corner of the cloisters, on the stone seat around the wall, can be seen various sets of nine holes; these were used for games played by pre-reformation schoolboys, using marbles which were rolled into the holes or for a game of 'jacks'.

In the opposite corner, through the Dark Passage, can be found the Museum in which there are many interesting items, including waxwork figures of Queen Anne and Lord Nelson.

Westminster Bridge was built with funds raised by a government-sponsored lottery. Opened on 17th November 1750 with a torchlight procession, it replaced a ferry (the compensation to the ferryman being £3,000) which in turn replaced a ford across the river dating from Roman times. When in 1846 the bridge was declared unsafe, due to the greater pressures brought about by the opening of the then new London Bridge, the structure was replaced in 1864 by the present bridge. At the Westminster end, under the shadow of Thornycroft's statue of Queen Boudicca, is a small copper-clad 'house' (19), containing a device for measuring the height of the tides on this stretch of the river. From 1906 to 1953 the bridge carried a double track for trams which makes it one of the widest bridges on the Thames with 84 feet between the parapets.

At the Lambeth end of Westminster Bridge now stands

the **Coade-stone lion** (20) from the brewery which was demolished at the time of the Festival of Britain.

On ground once known as **'Pedlar's Acre'** stands the former **County Hall** of London (21), which housed the administrative centre of the largest municipal authority in the world until the dissolution of the Greater London Council in 1986. The name may have been derived from a pedlar who bequeathed land to the parish of St Mary, Lambeth; one version of the story is that the pedlar and his dog were sheltering from a storm in the porch of the church and were both invited into vespers, the man later considered this the turning point of his life and as a thank-offering gave the land. Another story tells how the pedlar and his dog were sheltering near the ferry and the dog unearthed a treasure, and from his new-found wealth the pedlar gave the acre or, alternatively, that the bequest was made in order that the pedlar's dog could be buried in the churchyard.

Four centuries later the London County Council purchased the land from the parish for £81,000, but as the Parish Vestry had been superseded by Lambeth Borough Council it was to the latter that the money was eventually paid. A Roman boat was found when digging the foundations of the hall and is now in the possession of the Museum of London, London Wall. The architect of the riverside buildings of County Hall was Ralph Knott (1878-1929), and although they were opened in 1922 much of the present complex of buildings is of more recent date.

The building opposite County Hall in York Road was the **General Lying-in Hospital** for pregnant married women (22), founded by John Leake in 1765, and one of London's largest and earliest maternity hospitals, dating from the eighteenth century.

The former headquarters of the Metropolitan Police, **New and Old Scotland Yard** (23), were built on the foundations of a proposed national opera house, the rooms below ground level being the extent of the building.

In 1691 Queen Mary II had alterations made to the river front of **Whitehall Palace** when Wren built a new terrace and during excavations for the Ministry of Defence buildings the stairs were uncovered (24).

To celebrate the centenary of the Great Exhibition, the Festival of Britain was held in 1951. Bordered by County Hall on the west side and Waterloo Bridge on the other, the Festival Site, now known as **South Bank,** has been developed into a cultural centre. The immense tower block of **the Shell Petroleum Company (25), completed in 1962, is about 351 feet high and has seven thousand windows.**

In 1769 the Coade family set up business on the site now

occupied by the **Royal Festival Hall** (26). Their artificial stone was both cheap and durable; the formula was based on a patent of 1722 and was used by two other 'men of Lambeth' but needed the added 'something' of the Coade family. The secret died with the family and has resisted all attempts at analysis over the years. A grinding-stone, found in 1951, is now displayed in front of the hall on the lower level. Ironically, Coade Stone has stood up to the atmosphere of London better than any natural stone. Examples can be seen in the keystones of Queen Anne's Gate.

Today **York House Watergate** (27) stands marooned from the river it was built to serve; originally the riverside entrance to York House, it was designed by Inigo Jones with carvings by Nicholas Stone, and it has stood here since the early seventeenth century.

A flight of steps beside the watergate leads to Buckingham Street. Number 15, where both Dickens and David Copperfield lodged, has gone but a plaque marks the house to which the diarist Samuel Pepys came in 1679 after fire had destroyed his house near Tower Hill.

In **Carting Lane,** which links the Strand with the Embankment, stands a gas lamp (28) that never goes out—it is lit from the gases in the sewers underneath the streets of London.

To the side of the Institute of Electrical Engineers at the foot of **Savoy Hill** (29) stands London's first all-green public telephone box; until a recent rearrangement of the garden it was, quite literally, in a tree, having a hawthorn tree draped over it. Apparently the Institute objected to the box's colour (at that time all GPO boxes were red) on the grounds that it would clash with their building!

Prior to the building of the **Victoria Embankment** by Bazalgette between 1862 and 1870, the river came up to the walls of **Somerset House** (30), the wide arches along this side of the building being the watergate entrances.

Formerly a sloop of the Royal Navy, the **Wellington** (32) is now the floating livery hall of the Honourable Company of Master Mariners. The staircase was part of the former Isle of Man and Clyde trading ship *Viper*. The hall is unique and is the only company hall outside the City, having been moored here since 1948 when it was brought from Chatham Dockyard.

Marking the boundary of the City of London are the dragons of the City's arms (33). This stretch of water is known as the **King's Reach** and commemorates the Silver Jubilee of King George V in 1935; a tablet in the embankment wall commemorates the event.

Sir Arthur Blomfield, architect of the 'new' nave of Southwark Cathedral designed **Sion College** (34), which was completed in 1886. It contains a theological library and also acts as a social centre for the clergy of London. Founded in 1623 as a college and almshouse on London Wall, it was moved here on completion of the new buildings. The college now houses the City Livery Club.

Blackfriars Station (35) has now been entirely rebuilt on its original site, but the intriguing facade of the old station has not been replaced. On the former entrance were such enticing names as St Petersburg, Vienna and Wiesbaden, but it is a long time since one could book to these places from here.

Beside the **Mermaid Theatre** (36) once was found **Puddle Dock,** named either after an owner or from the fact that it was used as a watering place for horses. The name figures in several literary works: in *Bartholomew Fair* (1616) by Ben Jonson (1574-1637); Dean Swift (1667-1745) has a Countess of Puddle Dock in *Polite Conversation;* and William Hogarth (1697-1764) introduces a Duke of Puddle Dock in his *Trip to Gravesend.* The dock also became synonymous with low life and criminal activities.

Opened in 1959 by the Lord Mayor of London, the Mermaid was the first theatre sanctioned by the City for three hundred years. When new office blocks were built on the site in 1978-81 the theatre was incorporated as a condition for building and it reopened, enlarged and modernised, in 1981.

On the site where until 1974 *The Times* newspaper, which was founded in 1785, was printed a modern banking office stands over the former **Printing House Square** (37); under the building are the scattered remains of Blackfriars Monastery. St Dominic was a Spaniard by birth, a canon of Osma and described as being a man of fiery and impetuous temper who would not tolerate sects within the Church. In 1215 he obtained approval from Pope Innocent III to set up a new monastic order — the Order of Preachers, or 'Dominicans'. Based originally on the rules of St Augustine of Hippo and later additions, the order became very strict in its observance of absolute poverty. Established in Oxford by the second decade of the thirteenth century, and soon after in London, by 1276 they had grown to such an extent that they were given two whole streets where they might erect new buildings. At the Dissolution, in 1539, the church was given to St Anne's parish. Little remains above ground today although, in a former churchyard of St Anne's, off Ireland Yard, can be seen a small portion of the wall of the Provinicial's Hall.

Leading from Carter Lane to Playhouse Yard is **Church Entry** (38) which marks the division between the nave and the choir of the church of the Blackfriars. During digging operations in 1926 workmen uncovered a small part of the choir which showed signs of having been badly burned—could this have been during the Great Fire of London? Some of the stones and some human remains were transferred to St Dominic's Priory, Haverstock Hill, in North London where the latter were given a formal burial; however, the remains of one skeleton, found in the north-east corner of Church Entry, was left behind. It had been buried, presumably in medieval times, without a coffin and with only a plain board over the grave; in addition the skull had been broken with a blunt instrument—perhaps a monastic murder? St Anne's Vestry building was designed by Bannister Fletcher and Sons, the father being the author of the famous architectural history book *A Study of Architecture by the Comparative Method.*

Playhouse Yard marks the site of the Blackfriars Theatre (39) which was erected in the refectory of the former monastic buildings. It was used by Shakespeare and other theatrical companies as a winter theatre, as the open-air theatres on Bankside, Southwark, were not suitable for performances in inclement weather, whereas this large assembly hall could be used at all times. In 1576 Richard Farrant acquired the lease of 'six upper chambers, lofts and lodgings and other rooms lying together within the precinct of the late dissolved house or priory of the Blackfriars'. Originally the theatre was a private one for members only, but later it opened for public performances. During the latter stages of its life there were constant complaints by the local residents of the behaviour of the audiences; among the causes for complaint were the clapping of hands, destruction of local stallholders' property, and the wearing of sweaty nightcaps!

One of the knights who came over to England with William the Conqueror built **Baynard's Castle** (40) on a site by the then riverbank, where St Andrew's Hill stands today. At the beginning of the thirteenth century it came into the possession of Robert Fitzwalter, the hereditary banner-bearer of the City of London, and because he sided with the barons against King John at the sealing of Magna Carta in 1215 it was destroyed. With the coming of the Blackfriars the castle was moved to the river's edge to a site near the Mermaid Theatre. During the redevelopment of the area in the 1970s the whole area was explored and much useful information about the castle was discovered; the movable fragments are in the possession of the Museum of London in the Barbican.

One of the oldest hithes (inlets on the river bank where goods could be safely unloaded), **Queenhithe** (41) was first used in Roman times but was later abandoned by larger craft, as London Bridge made it impossible for them to pass into the upper reaches of the Thames. In the twelfth century it was primarily used by the Hanseatic League (see under Cannon Street Station).

One of the twelve Great Companies of the City, the Vintners, was first incorporated in 1437 although they existed at least two hundred years before that. Until 1552 they were responsible for the licences of all inns throughout England. The **Vintners' Hall** (42), except for the Court Room, was destroyed in the Great Fire and rebuilt in 1671. Commemorating an occasion in the fourteenth century when five kings sat down at their banquet (the monarchs of England, Scotland, France, Cyprus and Denmark) the loyal toast at annual dinners is cheered five times instead of the normal three. On the side of the building can be seen a Coade-stone figure of a blue-coated boy of the Vintners' School. With the Dyers' Company the Vintners have the privilege of owning swans on the Thames; every July the two companies go 'swan-upping'—catching the young cygnets and notching their beaks with one notch for the Dyers' birds, and two for the Vintners'. All unmarked birds belong to the Queen. This ceremony is also the origin of the inn sign the 'Swan with Two Necks', which should be 'two nicks' although a two-headed swan is shown over the entrance to the Hall in Upper Thames Street.

Cannon Street Station (43) is on the site of the Steelyard (a corruption of the word *stapel-hof*, meaning 'heap of merchandise') where the Easterlings, North German Baltic Coast merchants, set up business between the tenth and sixteenth centuries. Also known as the Hanseatic League, they gave this country its currency values, i.e. sterling.

Bankside, Southwark, today presents a wide variety of buildings ranging from private houses to warehouses. On the outside of one residence (44) is a plaster plaque stating 'Wren lived here . . .' Although the present building, externally at least, is later than Wren's time, it is conceivable that he lived on Bankside in the late seventeenth century when so much of his time was devoted to plans for rebuilding the City, but there is no documentary evidence to support the claim.

The office development in the area of Rose Alley and Park Street, very close to Southwark Bridge, is built over the excavation of the Elizabethan Rose Theatre. It opened in the autumn of 1587 and Shakespeare's *Henry VI, Part I* probably had its first production there. The lease of the building ran out in 1605 and it was pulled down in 1606.

Further along Bankside the northern boundary wall of a former brewery site bears a plaque showing Shakespeare and a bas-relief of Southwark and its theatres. Beyond the wall, just before Bankside meets Park Street, is the site of the **Globe Theatre** (45) built in 1599 by Cuthbert Burbage with timbers from The Theatre, the first theatre in London, which opened in 1577. The Globe survived until the theatres were closed by Parliament in 1642 in the Civil War. It was pulled down in 1644.

Clink Street (46) is a reminder of the Clink (prison) which used to form part of the Bishop of Winchester's complex. The prison was mainly used to house heretics and other offenders against the Church.

Near Clink Street is **St Mary Overies Dock,** another of the ancient hithes of London, where, since the sixteenth century, parishioners of St Saviour's, Southwark, have been entitled to land goods free of toll. The suffix 'Overy' or 'Overie' is said to have derived from 'over the river', a medieval title to differentiate Southwark's church dedicated to St Mary from others. It could also commemorate a ferryman who plied for business along this stretch of the river, whose name was Overie. In order to find out the true feelings of his family towards himself, and to ascertain whether one of his daughters would marry a certain man of whom her father did not approve, he pretended to die. His family were so pleased, that after having laid him in his coffin complete with shroud, they proceeded to have a party in the next room. Overie was not amused at the event and promptly left his coffin and entered the room where the jollifications were taking place. The daughter's boy-friend, seeing what he thought was a ghost, struck out at the advancing figure—who promptly fell down dead; this time, after they had laid him in his coffin, he stayed there, and the party was resumed.

Founded originally as St Mary-over-the-River—St Mary Overie—the present day **Cathedral of Southwark** (47) became a parish church after being an Augustinian priory for over four hundred years, and in 1905 it was raised to the dignity of a cathedral. John Harvard, founder of Harvard University in America, was baptised here; today St John's Chapel is known as the Harvard Chapel and is maintained by the university. The stone reredos behind the high altar is virtually a history book in stone with the figures representing persons connected with Southwark through the ages. In the entrance lobby to one of the vestries can be seen a very rare twelfth-century consecration cross, inscribed in 1107. Just outside the south-west doorway is some Roman herringbone walling, while at the west end of the south choir aisle is an example of Roman tessellated pavement.

London Bridge (48), officially opened by the Queen in March 1973, is the fifth bridge to cross the Thames at, or near, this point. The nineteenth-century bridge, designed by Rennie and opened in 1832, was sold in 1969 for one million pounds and is now in Arizona, USA. When the bridge was demolished the Nancy steps disappeared. Here Bill Sykes, in Dickens's *Oliver Twist,* overheard a conversation that led to Nancy's being murdered by him in a north London house.

Appropriately sited at the north end of London Bridge is the **Company Hall of the Worshipful Company of Fishmongers** of London (49). Among the many exhibits in the hall is a chair made from the wood of the medieval London Bridge.

In the forecourt of the church of **St Magnus the Martyr** (50) are some pieces of the medieval London Bridge as well as a piece of the nineteenth-century one.

In 1699 a charter was granted to **Billingsgate** and it remained the official fish market of the City of London until 1982. It has been rebuilt several times, the last rebuilding being in 1876 by Horace Jones. The fish-porters wore billy-cocks, a special kind of helmet, when carrying the trays of fish: modelled on the leather helmets worn by the bowmen at the battle of Agincourt, they were made entirely out of leather weighing about five pounds and were practically indestructible, being passed down from father to son as family heirlooms. The fish market is now at West India Docks.

The **Customs House** standing next to Billingsgate Market (51) was a place of near tragedy for English literature. Here the poet William Cowper tried to drown himself in the river —but the tide was out at the time!

Rivalling 'Speakers Corner' in Hyde Park, Tower Hill at the east end of **All Hallows Church** (52) also has its fair share of lunch-time orators. While at other times in the day the 'buskers'—street performers—demonstrate their escaping tricks for the amusement of the crowds.

At the foot of Tower Hill stands the **Tower Subway Kiosk** (53) which in 1869 was the entrance to London's first railway under the Thames; the journey took a few minutes from here to its other outlet in Southwark. With the opening of Tower Bridge in 1894 the subway became redundant although it was used by pedestrians for a short time. Today it houses cables and other vital lifelines of communication.

Countless hundreds of men and women have been publicly executed on Tower Hill, and the execution scaffold site draws crowds of interested tourists to the spot today (54). The first of the inscribed names is Simon of Sudbury, the Archbishop of Canterbury who was beheaded by Wat Tyler, the insurrectionist, in 1381 after being dragged from the Tower by the rebels. For his part in the Jacobite Rising of 1745 Simon Fraser, Lord Lovat, was executed in 1747—the last public beheading on Tower Hill.

Built to protect the City of London by William the Conqueror (1066-1087) the **Tower of London** (55), or more correctly Her Majesty's Royal Palace and Fortress of the Tower of London, is today one of the most popular tourist attractions of London. But, like so many other well-visited places, it has items of curiosity value that may be missed by many people. Traitors' Gate built in the thirteenth century and spanning 61 feet has no key-stone, the wedge-shaped stone which usually holds the arch in position. On either side of the archway under the Bloody Tower—more correctly The Garden Tower—is a semi-circular iron rail with spikes on it: it is said that the Duke of Wellington, returning to the Tower after a late party, found the guard asleep in the corner —that is no longer possible!

One of the twenty or more monastic establishments in London at the time of the Dissolution of the Monasteries, *c.* 1540, was **St Katherine's** which had been founded by Queen Matilda, wife of King Stephen, in 1148. In 1825 a scheme planned by the St Katherine's Dock Board was put into being and the dock was constructed on the site of the Precinct (56). The area has been transformed into a leisure centre, with a hotel and eating and drinking places. The marina is full of boats throughout the year.

3. LAWYERS' LONDON

Founded in the fourteenth century, **Gray's Inn** (1) occupies land where the mansion of Lord Grey de Wilton once stood. After his death in 1308 the property was left vacant until the Society of Gray's Inn was formed. One tree in the garden is said to have been planted by Sir Francis Bacon who laid out the gardens in the seventeenth century. The gatehouse, first built in 1594, and rebuilt in 1964-1965, leads into High Holborn. Shakespeare's *Comedy of Errors* was first performed in the Hall of the Inn in 1594.

At **Henekey's Wine House** in High Holborn (2) there is a yard glass—the idea is to see if you can drink it all down in one go, or without pausing for breath or spilling it over the floor. The fireplace in the centre of the bar appears to have no chimney—the smoke being diverted under the floor.

At the junction of Gray's Inn Road and High Holborn stands **Holborn Bars** (3); this is one of a series of outer 'gates' set some distance from the City walls. Although they are not fortified gates one might liken the bars to the frontier posts where tolls and commercial dues could be collected. The keepers of the bars could also scrutinise persons entering the city and perhaps turn away those who were suffering from a contagious disease.

An 'inn', strictly interpreted, is a place where lodgings, as well as food, can be had. In the fourteenth century the Wool Staplers (wool merchants) settled at Holborn Bars and, naturally, their inn became **Staple Inn.** Today the front presents a glimpse of the London of the late Middle Ages. In order to pay for his mother's funeral Dr Samuel Johnson, who lived here between 1759 and 1760, wrote *Rasselas.*

The Prudential Assurance Company's building, designed by Alfred Waterhouse, is on the site of **Furnivall's Inn** (4), another vanished Inn of Court. Charles Dickens had chambers here from 1834 to 1837 until the birth of his first child, when he and his young wife, Catherine Hogarth, moved to 48 Doughty Street.

In the thirteenth century the Bishops of Ely built their palace here, comprising a very fine complex of rooms (5). The land is extra-parochial as far as the rest of London is concerned, having its own beadle to maintain order, who up to the outbreak of the Second World War used to patrol

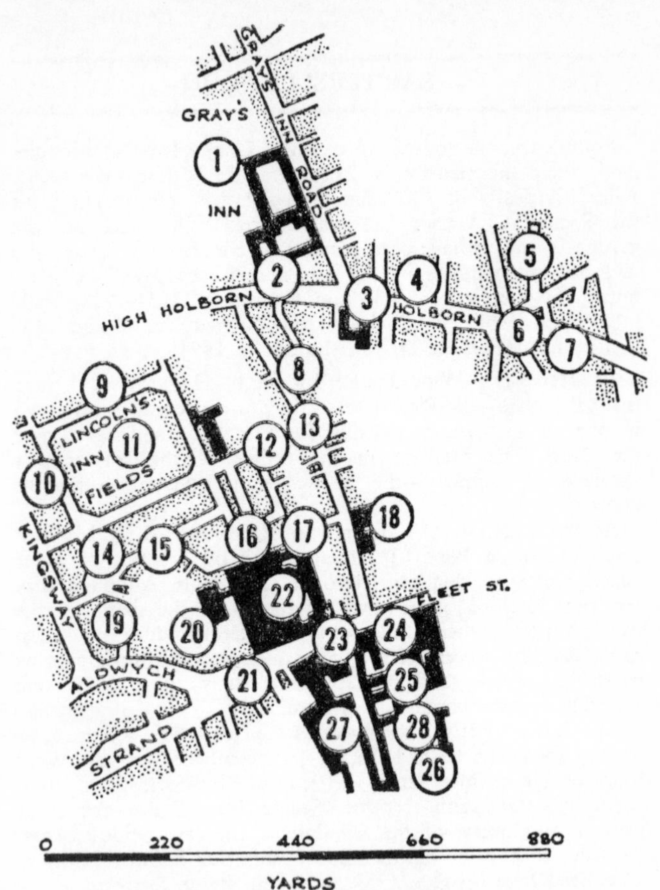

LAWYERS' LONDON

1. Gray's Inn
2. Henekey's Wine House
3. Holborn Bars
4. Furnivall's Inn site
5. Palace of Bishops of Ely
6. Statue of Prince Albert
7. City Temple
8. London Silver Vaults
9. Soane's Museum
10. 59-60 Lincoln's Inn Fields
11. Execution plaque
12. Lincoln's Inn chapel
13. Lincoln's Inn cellar
14. Old Curiosity Shop
15. Portugal Street
16. Thomas More memorial
17. Carey Street boundary stones
18. Public Records Office
19. Clare Market
20. The Anchorage
21. St Clement Danes
22. Royal Courts of Justice
23. Temple Bar
24. 17-18 Fleet Street
25. The Temple
26. Temple Gardens
27. Middle Temple Hall
28. Inner Temple

the street and called out the state of the weather and the time of night: 'Twelve of the clock on a misty night, and all's well'. The gates at the entrance are still locked every night, and no policeman patrols the street, only entering if specifically requested to do so.

At the roundabout is London's 'politest statue'—the seated figure of Prince Albert always raises his hat to passers-by (6). The work of Bacon, it represents Peace and Commerce in the Great Exhibition of 1851, and the laying of the foundation stone of the Royal Exchange in 1842 is depicted in the bas-reliefs around the pedestal.

The **City Temple** (7), the only English free church in the City of London, was originally founded in the late sixteenth century when services were probably held in the Plumbers Hall in Anchor Lane. The church on Holborn Viaduct was opened in 1874 and cost £70,000.

Lying deep underground at **53 Chancery Lane** (8) is the Aladdin's cave of London—the London Silver Vaults. Here you may come just to look at or to buy a complete cutlery set. Old and new silverware can be seen side by side.

In 1812-14 Sir John Soane, architect of the Bank of England, built three houses in Lincoln's Inn Fields (9), numbers 12 to 14. He set up house in number 13 and let the houses on either side. In his own house he gathered around himself and his family many items of architectural and artistic interest. Soane's disappointment that his sons did not follow him into the architectural profession led him to obtain an Act of Parliament to protect his collection, and the setting up of **Soane's Museum.** A visit to the museum will reveal, apart from the furnishings, a number of items of unusual interest: the face mask of Sarah Siddons, the famous eighteenth-century actress; arches from the old Palace of Westminster; the marble sarcophagus of Seti I which Soane brought from Egypt, hoping to sell it to the British Museum, which he failed to do, and so he retained it for his own collection. One of the greatest surprises is the Picture Room, measuring some ten feet square, which houses dozens of pictures hung on walls which open and close like cupboards. There are many of Soane's own drawings of commissioned work and competition entries. But perhaps the most important pictures of the room are those by William Hogarth, and depict the *Rake's Progress* and the *Election* series. Both series show life in the eighteenth century and are some of the finest satirical pictures of the Age of Reason. For serious architectural students the collection also includes drawings by the architects George Dance, Robert Adam and, of course, John Soane.

When Inigo Jones laid out **Lincoln's Inn Fields** in 1618 he designed a number of houses surrounding them; numbers 59-60 remain as examples of his work (10), and Charles Dickens came to read *The Chimes* next door at number 58 to some of his more intimate friends, prior to publication.

Since the late nineteenth century Lincoln's Inn Fields has been a public open space comprising some twelve acres. In the past the Fields have been a popular place for the fighting of duels. In the centre of the Fields Lord William Russell was executed in 1683 for his part in the Rye House Plot. A brass plaque under the shelter in the middle (11) records the execution.

A unique feature of the **Lincoln's Inn Chapel** (12), designed by Inigo Jones in the seventeenth century, is the open undercroft, where students and men of law can talk and walk.

Under the gatehouse, where each night the Head Porter rings the curfew at 9 p.m., is an old cellar with beautiful brickwork (13). The bell was brought from Spain by Lord Essex on one of his many trips abroad. Here too is the house in which Oliver Cromwell lived, and where he signed the death warrant of Charles I.

Of all the tourist attractions in London the **Old Curiosity Shop** (14) has raised the most controversy over the past years. There seems little doubt that while Dickens knew this shop—from his frequent visits to Lincoln's Inn Fields—the original building which inspired him stood where Irving Street and Charing Cross Road now meet. This will not, and should not, deter visitors from coming here to see an excellent example of a sixteenth-century shop with living quarters above it.

Here, in **Portugal Street** (15), were the last stocks used in London until 1826.

At the junction of Serle Street and Carey Street there is a memorial to **Saint Sir Thomas More** (1478-1535) (16), commemorating his connection with Lincoln's Inn. More was born in Milk Street in the City and was admitted to Lincoln's Inn in 1496, after which he became a member of Parliament, opposed Henry VII's demand for money, and as a consequence had to withdraw from public life. He came to the notice of Henry VIII and, after Cardinal Wolsey's fall from power, was appointed Lord Chancellor. Because of his strong religious beliefs he would not assist Henry VIII to obtain his divorce from Catherine of Aragon, and for refusing to accept the Oath of Supremacy he was committed to the Tower of London. Found guilty on these charges and of treason he was executed on 6th July 1535. He was canonised by the Roman Catholic Church in 1935.

In **Carey Street** are two stones (17) which mark the boundary of the two local parishes of St Clement Danes, in the Strand, and St Dunstan-in-the-West, Fleet Street. The former has an anchor-ring, and the latter the initials SDW reading anti-clockwise.

To the side of the boundary stones was a shop, first established in the seventeenth century, where ladies could purchase silver mouse-traps. As it was fashionable to powder the hair with flour, it is hardly surprising that mice nested in it. So, when going to bed at night, a silver mouse-trap was placed conveniently on a side table.

Until the establishment of the **Public Records Office** (18) by an Act of Parliament of 1838 the records and archives of the country were stored in the Tower of London. Since the building of the office—the Fetter Lane side dates from 1851-66—a unique collection of documents relating to the history of Britain has been housed there. Ranging from the Domesday Survey of 1086 to Parliamentary Writs and Returns of 1955, the office, one of the least visited museums in London, has much in it to interest the curiosity hunter.

Clare Market (19) is on land originally owned by the Earl of Clare and clients included the actors and actresses of Drury Lane. It also developed into a 'rookery'—a place where criminals set themselves up to form a commune—and was later the site of the St Clement Danes workhouse. Appropriately the former vicarage of St Clement Danes church is called **The Anchorage** (20).

Now the church of the Royal Air Force, **St Clement Danes** (21) was rebuilt by Sir Christopher Wren in 1680 and internally restored after its destruction by fire in the Second World War. St Clement was martyred, *c.* 100, by being attached to the anchor of a ship and thrown overboard; his sign, an anchor, can be seen on a number of buildings around the parish. The floor of the nave of the church is paved with inscribed slates depicting RAF crests.

At the City end of The Strand stand the **Royal Courts of Justice** (22), popularly known as the Law Courts, opened in 1882 by Queen Victoria and designed by George Edmund

Street. The Law Courts stand on land once owned by the Knights Templars, a military order of monks whose main purpose was to protect the holy places of Palestine, and their tilting-yard was also here.

Over the main entrance to the courts are three statues: to the left is Solomon, holding his Temple—the only perfect building ever erected, in deference to which fact many architects, Street included, never allowed their buildings to be absolutely completed, and there is an only partly carved column in the courts to bear witness to this; on the right is King Alfred the Great, law-giver to the English nation; and on the apex of the Great Hall's roof is Christ, His hand raised in blessing, the only secular building in London so blessed. At the other end of the hall, in Carey Street, stands Moses with the tablets of the Word—the Ten Commandments of the Old Testament. Each October the City of London presents two faggots cut with a billhook and six horseshoes with sixty-one nails to the Queen's Remembrancer. The former represents rent for The Moors in Shropshire and the latter for the forge in St Clement Danes parish. The same nails and shoes have been offered for five hundred years! Furthermore, nobody is quite sure where The Moors is, or whether the forge existed at all. There was, until 1932, however, a smithy owned by W. H. Smith's, the booksellers, in a nearby street called Tweezers Alley.

The site of **Temple Bar** (23) is marked by a monument showing Queen Victoria and various bas-reliefs which include one of Wren's Temple Bar. While never a fortified entrance to the City of London Temple Bar marks the City limits of jurisdiction. Here the monarch is stopped by City officials when visiting the City. The keys of London and the Sword of State are offered to the monarch, who returns them if he or she comes in peace. Prior to its removal in the nineteenth century, Wren's gatehouse was used by the nearby Child's Bank as a depository for its archives, while in the days of decapitation, heads were frequently displayed over the roof, doubtless as a deterrent to would-be criminals entering the City. One man used to make his living by hiring spy-glasses, at a farthing a time, so that the curious could obtain a better view of the skulls.

The Automobile Association was founded in 1905 at **18 Fleet Street** (24) by a group of motoring enthusiasts in order to protect the road-users of the time from persecution by the police. As a part of its diamond jubilee celebrations on 18th

June 1965 a plaque was unveiled on the present building by the Lord Mayor of London, Sir James Miller.

Early in the seventeenth century the Council of the Duchy of Cornwall built a house at **17 Fleet Street** (24). Used as its council chamber, it displays, in its very fine ceilings, the fleur-de-lis of the Prince of Wales, and the initials PH, those of Prince Henry, James I's elder son, whose death before his father in 1612 left his younger brother to succeed to the throne as Charles I. The gardens of the **Temple** (25) are world-famous for the roses that grow there, and were the scene of the plucking of the roses, one white (York) and one red (Lancaster), that saw the beginning of the Wars of the Roses in the fifteenth century. Also in the gardens is the statue of a kneeling Moor who balances a sun-dial on his head. The Earl of Clare brought it back to this country after a visit to Italy in the seventeenth century and gave it to Clement's Inn after his Indian servant had murdered one of the students. At that time the inn was in Fleet Street, where today a block of flats stands, and after the demolition of the inn it was bought by a private individual and given to the Inner Temple.

For the curious or the literary explorer, **Temple Gardens** (25-26) can offer many items of interest. Fountain Court, with its fountain standing in the centre, reminds us of Ruth Pinch and her brother Tom meeting here; also Pump Court was where Tom Pinch acted as librarian; Mr Pip and his friend Herbert Pocket lived in Garden Court in *Great Expectations;* while Paper Buildings has its memories of Sir John Chester in *Barnaby Rudge* and the chambers of Mr Stryver KC of the *Tale of Two Cities.*

Middle Temple Hall (27) was built in 1574 and is one of the finest Tudor halls in England. The table is reputed to have been made from the wood of Drake's *Golden Hind,* but both Middle Temple and Gray's Inn claim him as a member. In term time, every evening, a horn is blown from the steps of the hall summoning the Benchers to dinner. The badge of the Middle Temple is the Agnus Dei (the lamb with the nimbus and banner, with a red cross on a white background) and the device of the **Inner Temple** (28) is Pegasus, the winged horse, and can be seen on buildings around the Temple.

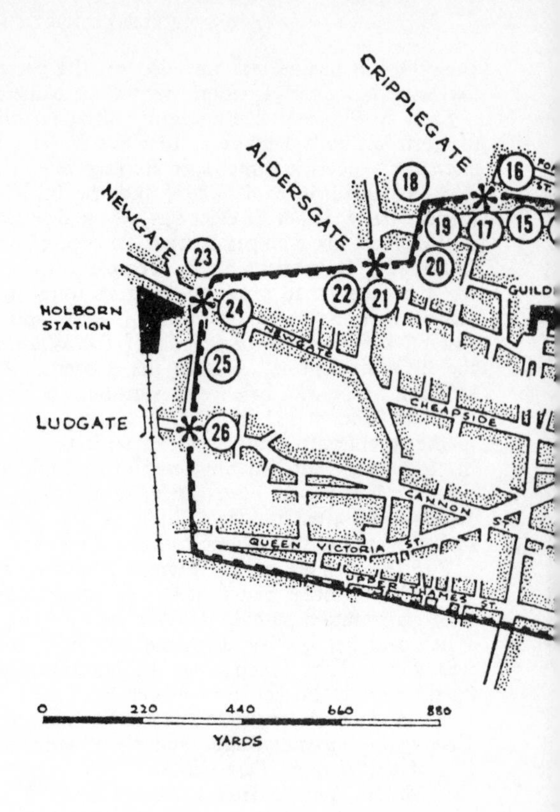

ENCLOSED BY A CITY WALL

1. Tower of London
2. Tower Hill station
3. Toc H House
4. Sir John Cass College
5. Aldgate Pump
6. Mitre Square
7. Spanish and Portuguese Synagogue
8. Bishopsgate
9. All Hallows, London Wall
10. Carpenters' Hall
11. Moorfields
12. Moorgate
13. Moor House
14. Elsing Priory
15. St Alphage's, London Wall
16. Roman House
17. Cripplegate
18. St Giles's, Cripplegate
19. Roman Fort
20. Noble Street
21. Aldersgate
22. Bull and Mouth Inn
23. Giltspur Street
24. Newgate
25. Central Criminal Courts
26. Ludgate

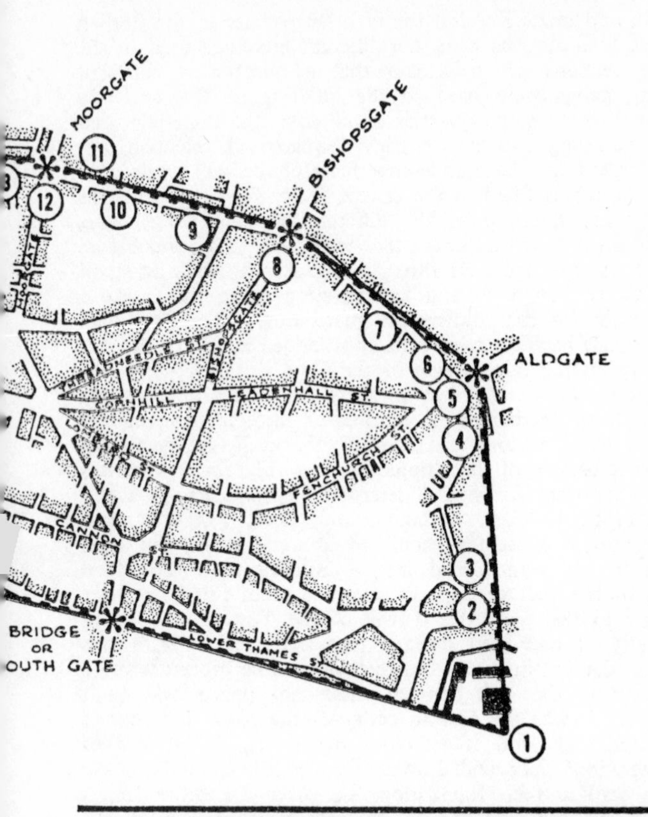

4. ENCLOSED BY A CITY WALL

The history of London's city wall begins in the second century A.D., although the experts cannot agree as to exactly when it was built. One school of thought dates the wall from about A.D. 140, while another puts its building as late as A.D. 190—it was certainly not built earlier as history records that in A.D. 60-61 Queen Boudicca razed Londinium (the Roman name for the City) to the ground, as a reprisal against the Romans who had assaulted her daughters and confiscated her lands on the death of her husband Prasutagus, king of the Iceni tribe. When completed, the wall enclosed some 330 acres of land, and made London the fifth largest city in the Roman Empire. It is obvious from the different bondings used in the various sections which remain that a number of different building gangs were used in the building of the wall. As London had no stone quarries of its own, the materials used had to be brought in from outside: 'squared-off' Kentish ragstone formed the inner and outer faces of the wall while concrete and rubble filled in the centre. Every few feet (and this is the main variation of the different building gangs) one, two, or three rows of Roman tiles were used as a bond before proceeding with the next three to five feet of wall. It stood about thirty feet high, and had running along the inside a sentry walk for the soldiers on guard duty; at a later date semi-circular bastions were built as an added means of defence—mainly on the eastern side of the City, this being the side most prone to attack from invaders or pirates approaching London from down-river. A number of these towers can still be seen along various stretches of the wall, in particular the corner bastion of the Cripplegate fort. The main entrances to the City were Aldgate, Aldersgate, Newgate, Ludgate and Bridge or South Gate. Without a wall London was an open city, a port, a place for people to live and work, but with a wall it was transformed into a military post. The final stretch of the wall to be built stretched from the Blackfriars of today to the Wardrobe Tower of the Tower of London. Originally, it had been decided that the river Thames was sufficient defence in itself—but they were to be proved wrong! Consequently the wall between these two points was built (ironically it was the first to collapse—the river undermined the foundations and it fell into the river). A number of buildings in Upper and Lower Thames Streets today have Roman wall as their foundation. To cover the entire length of the completed wall one has to walk over three miles, but there are so many interesting places to visit on the way that the time soon passes.

To many visitors to the **Tower of London** (1) the ruins at the south-east corner of the White Tower are merely something to hurry past on the way out, but to others they are the beginning of London Wall. In fact, they formed part of a bastion on the corner of the wall, and were later adapted to form part of the Wardrobe Tower of the King's Royal Palace at the Tower. Examination of the remains reveals Roman and later work in their construction.

Travellers arriving by Underground to visit the Tower of

London can find remains of the city wall on Platform 1 of Tower Hill Station. It was revealed when the present station was being built in 1967, while just outside the station (2) can be seen a fine stretch of the Roman wall and the later wall of the City. Here is one of London's earliest inscribed monuments, which commemorates the Procurator of Britain — the Financial Officer — between A.D. 61 and 65. He pacified the rebellions against Roman rule, including Queen Boudicca's. The original inscription is in the British Museum and it will be noticed that there are still some parts missing; during the building of a sub-power station nearby these portions were found about sixteen to eighteen feet below the present-day surface. It must be remembered that we add about one foot of rubble to the level of our cities each century, therefore the Roman level is quite a long way down, but standing by the side of the foundations of the gate gives one an idea of the height and structure of the wall.

In the north-east corner of Tower Hill was **Toc H House,** the home of the interdenominational organisation founded by the late Rev. 'Tubby' P. B. Clayton in the First World War; behind it is an excellent stretch of London Wall (3). The organisation gets its name from Talbot House—Toc H in signallers' language—and was started on the Flanders battle-field at Poperinghe, six miles from Ypres. On the wall at the side of the house is a painting showing Coopers Row as it was during the Middle Ages when it was known as Woodruffe Lane from the surname of the owner of the land, in turn derived from an English woodland flower. It was renamed in 1750 when the coopers (barrel makers) were prominent in this area. Coopers Row runs parallel to the wall and behind a modern office building (3) can be seen a fine stretch of exposed wall. The construction of the Roman and medieval wall, with the remains of a staircase and later windows, gives an excellent example of the wall at its prime. Passing through a modern postern gate one sees the formidable thirty feet of masonry which formed the outer side. A diagram on the side wall shows the route of the wall and the position of the bastions or rounded towers that were added later to strengthen the defence of the City. It was by using these towers that it was possible to survey the area without making oneself visible to attackers.

In Jewry Street stands the **Sir John Cass College** (4), founded in 1710 as the Sir John Cass's Foundation, which was for many years the only place in the City for advanced scientific study. On the wall are several plaques denoting ownership by the City of London (see the coat of arms of the City); others are the parish boundary marks of St Botolph, Aldgate, while another, with a wheel on it, shows the boundary of St Katharine Cree, and lastly there is the Ward of Aldgate sign. As the name implies, Jewry Street was once one of the Jewish areas in London.

At the road junction where Leadenhall Street and Gracechurch Street join Aldgate stands the **Aldgate Pump** (5). Before the channelling of water into the City there was a series of pumps and conduits from which water could be drawn. The present pump is a few yards away from where its predecessor stood and water from this pump had a different taste from other local pumps and efforts were made to trace the source; it was discovered that during its journey underground from the hills of Hampstead and Highgate it passed through a cemetery.

Between **Aldgate** (5) and **Bishopsgate** (8) the ditch which ran along the outside of the wall became known as **Houndsditch** from the number of dead dogs left there to rot in the Middle Ages.

One of the largest monastic establishments of pre-Reformation London was Holy Trinity, Aldgate, belonging to the Order of Augustinian Canons; only an arch or two remains but **Mitre Square** (6) is on the site of the cloisters of the abbey. It is also the site of one of the last known murders of Jack the Ripper in London.

The **Spanish and Portuguese Synagogue** (7) in Bevis Marks was first built in 1701. The architect was Mr Avis, a Quaker, who returned his fees to the synagogue as a gesture of goodwill. Queen Anne gave a beam for the roof. Much of the internal fittings, including the Tebah, were added *c.* 1730. Seven chandeliers were made in Amsterdam while a pair of scroll mounts date from the late seventeenth century. The street in which the synagogue is situated—Bevis Marks —derives its name from the fact that the Abbots of Bury St Edmunds had a house here prior to the Dissolution of the Monasteries.

The seventh-century Bishop of London, Saint Erkenwald, originally built **Bishopsgate** (8) and used to exact a toll of one piece of wood from all carts loaded with wood coming into the City. Later the maintenance of the gate became the responsibility of the Hanseatic merchants and in return they were allowed certain privileges within the City; however, until 1318 the Bishop was still responsible for the upkeep of the hinges. It was the merchants who in 1471 rebuilt the gate which lasted until the eighteenth century when it shared the fate of the other seven gates and was demolished and sold as scrap. Drawings show the upper storeys to be windowless and so uninhabitable. The building now on the site of the gate has a stone mitre carved on it.

The church of **All Hallows, London Wall** (9), is built at the side of and over the City wall.

Founded in 1333, incorporated in 1477, the **Worshipful Company of Carpenters** first built a hall here (10) in 1428. A land mine in May 1941 wrecked the hall and an explosion from gas mains in nearby London Wall completed the destruction. The company's records, charters, ordinances and furniture were saved, as was the Master's Garland, but the hall had to be rebuilt. The keystones of the arches at street level all portray famous architects and include William of Wykeham, Wren, Soane, Inigo Jones and Vanbrugh.

In 1246 a priory was set up outside the City wall and 'divided from Moorfields by a deep ditch'. By 1402 it had become a hospital for lunatics, who, according to Stowe, were transferred from a hospice at Charing Cross as the king didn't like it so near his palace! In 1675 the asylum was rebuilt in **Moorfields** (11), now Moorgate, and was designed by Robert Hooke, with a lease of 999 years from the Corporation of London, and an annual rent, if demanded, of one shilling. It stood 40 feet high and 540 feet long and was surrounded by a high wall.

Moorgate (12) is a major gateway into the City and dates from 1415 when Thomas Falconer, Lord Mayor of London, had the gate built. The area *outside* the wall, Moorfields, was used in the Middle Ages for recreational purposes. The river Walbrook starts its journey through the City from the fields and in winter overflowed and froze so making London's first open-air ice-rink. The apprentices tied the bones of animals to the soles of their shoes and used them as skates.

At the entrance to **Moor House** (13) is a dimensional mosaic that depicts the wall, with all the pieces of armour required by a Roman soldier. Using the upper walkway between Moorgate and Cripplegate one sees the redevelopment of London Wall after the devastation of the Blitz of 1940-41.

In the fourteenth century Sir John Elsing founded **Elsing Priory** (14) for one hundred blind men. At the Dissolution the inhabitants were turned out and the buildings sold; the domestic buildings were used as a house until a fire later in the sixteenth century destroyed them. Due to the bad state of repair of the church of **St Alphage, London Wall** (15) the congregation moved into the chapel of the priory. All that remains of the chapel today is the central crossing.

Nestling down among the buildings of modern London is a magnificent stretch of London Wall (15). By descending the staircase beside it one comes to a pleasant oasis and also gets an impression of the height and formidable approach of the wall to anyone attempting to scale it. Standing here, in what would have been the city ditch, it is easy to see how impenetrable the wall was in the Middle Ages. The lower portion is the *upper* part of the Roman wall, with medieval walling above, and capped by Tudor brickwork. The wall was kept in good repair after gunpowder made such defences superfluous and was used by the citizens as a means of getting quickly about the City; it was easier, and safer, to use the wall as a by-pass than to risk health and safety by walking through the narrow, often stinking streets and alleys.

Bestriding London Wall at Cripplegate, **Roman House** (16) offers two items of interest to the inquiring mind. The first is an inscribed stone in Fore Street commemorating the falling of the first explosive bomb of the Second World War, while in the foyer of the house is a mural on the wall showing Roman London.

Cripplegate (17) was once a gate into the military compound or fort of London, but was later enlarged to become a city gate. The name is derived from *crepel,* an Anglo-Saxon word for 'den' or 'underground passage'. Once the City gates were closed for the night, after the curfew had been rung, it was impossible to get into the City through any of the gateways, but here, at Cripplegate, was an underpass which enabled persons able to prove their identity to enter.

In the churchyard of **St Giles's, Cripplegate** (18), stands the corner bastion of the Roman fort, and of the City Wall. Excavation and rebuilding in the area of Cripplegate brought to light the guard room of the Roman fort (19). Between 12.30 and 14.00 on Mondays to Fridays one may visit the excavations.

Following excavations after the bombing of the Second World War a stretch of wall was uncovered in **Noble Street** (20). The results were to establish the line of the wall and lead to the discovery of the Roman fort. At the Gresham Street end of the site can be seen the foundations of the City wall, disappearing under the churchyard of St Anne and St Agnes Church, and the wall of the fort. Note particularly the remains of a guard tower which formerly stood on the corner of the fort.

When the city wall was first built, **Aldersgate** (21) became the north gate and as such became the 'Older-gate'. (An alternative derivation is that a man called Ealdred may have been responsible for its rebuilding at some time.) A document of 1289 specifically mentions Aldersgate and it certainly would have been concerned with the order of 1282 which read: 'All the gates of the city are to be open by day: and at each gate there are to be two sergeants to open the same, skilful men, and fluent of speech, who are to keep watch on persons coming and going so that no evil befall the City'. A later order, of the fourteenth century, says that each gate should have twelve men by day and twenty-four by night—'able-bodied, well instructed and well armed'. The gate was rebuilt in 1617 to the design of Gerald Christmas, the architect of nearby Northumberland House—its site is marked by a plaque. On the outer face of the gate was an equestrian statue of James I (VI of Scotland), who rode through its predecessor on coming to London to claim the throne of England. Until the Great Fire of London in 1666 the king's statue was flanked by the prophets Jeremiah and Samuel but these were replaced in 1672 by a boy and a girl. Judging by the picture on the churchyard wall—in Little Britain—the gateway, three storeys high, formed an impressive entrance to the City. It was at a later date used by a printer named John Day who would awaken his apprentices by calling out to them 'Awake for it is Day!'

Almost opposite the blue plaque which marks the site of Aldersgate is another plaque marking the former site of the **Bull and Mouth Inn** (22). When the Post Office bought the land here they demolished the inn, but the inn sign, a black bull with a large human mouth at its feet, can still be seen in the Museum of London.

Under the forecourt of the Post Office Building in Giltspur Street can be seen (after obtaining advance permission from the Post Office in King Edward Street) a corner bastion of the wall (23). Also on the nearby wall can be seen a blue plaque commemorating the site of the Giltspur Street Compter. A compter was a small prison, often just a house where persons could be detained for a supposedly short period of time. Many compters were so overcrowded that often ten times the number they were designed to hold were housed in them.

One of the oldest gateways into the City (traces of the Roman west gate of the city were found in 1874), **Newgate** (24) has become synonymous with the prison that started in the rooms over the gate. Rebuilt after being damaged in the Great Fire, Newgate was first used as a prison in the eleventh century.

Much damage was done to it during the Peasants' Revolt of 1381, which ended when the rebel leader, Wat Tyler, was stabbed to death by the Lord Mayor of London, Sir William Walworth; the alleged weapon is now held by the Fishmonger's Company in their hall in Upper Thames Street. Money left for charitable purposes by Richard Whittington, four times Lord Mayor of London, was used to repair the prison. After the 'No Popery Riots' of 1780 George Dance the Younger designed a new complex of buildings, which although larger than its predecessor was often overcrowded. In 1831 the debtors' side of the prison, designed to hold 100, held 340 prisoners. A Select Commission on Prison Discipline of 1852 restricted its use to prisoners awaiting execution. In 1880 it ceased to be used as a prison, except during the sitting of the Central Criminal Courts, and was finally demolished early in this century. The last public execution, outside the debtors' doorway, was in May 1868, when Michael Barrett was hanged for his part in trying to blow up Clerken House of Detention, the remains of which are still under the Hugh Myddleton School in Clerkenwell.

The **Central Criminal Courts** (25) now stand on the site and 200 feet above street level stands the statue of Justice, without the usual blindfold, which twice a year is carefully cleaned. Over the main entrance to the Courts are the sculptured figures of Truth, Justice and the Recording Angel, while the inscription reads 'Defend the children of the poor and punish the wrongdoer', taken from Psalm 72, selected by the Dean of Westminster and approved by the Archbishop of Canterbury. In the main foyer of the Central Criminal Courts is the only statue of a woman to be found within the precincts of an English court of justice. Based on a painting by Gibson and modelled by A. Drury, RA, it is of Elizabeth Fry, the famous Quaker prison reformer born at Norwich in 1780 and who died in 1845.

Whether **Ludgate** (26) is as old a gate as Newgate is open to dispute, but remains of a cemetery have been found along the line of Fleet Street which suggests that there was a road here in Roman days. The Romans did not, as a rule, bury within the precincts of a city, but almost invariably by the side of roads. King Lud, a mythical king of Britain, is said to have founded London, which is in fact 'Lud's Town', in days too far back in history to be recorded. A statue of King Lud and his sons taken from the gate can be seen at the church of **St Dunstan-in-the-West**, Fleet Street. It should also be mentioned that in old English *ludgeat* means 'postern', or 'back doorway'.

5. CURIOSITIES OF CITY CHURCHES

The number of parishes in the City of London at the end of the Middle Ages has been conservatively estimated at between 120 and 130, of which some three dozen have survived. After the Great Fire of London fifty-three churches were rebuilt by Sir Christopher Wren, and since the seventeenth century twenty-one have been pulled down, mainly to make way for office buildings. But still today the cry is that there are too many churches within the 'one square mile', with its now vastly reduced population.

Of the original 120, eight medieval churches remain in the City. They are All-Hallows-by-the-Tower (interior rebuilt after the Second World War), St Olave's, Hart Street, St Helen's and St Ethelburga's in Bishopsgate, St Giles's, Cripplegate, St Sepulchre's without Newgate, St Andrew Undershaft and St Bartholomew the Great.

Add to the above the thirty-five churches which were not rebuilt by Wren after the Great Fire, including St Botolph's, Aldersgate, St Botolph's, Bishopsgate, and St Botolph's, Aldgate, which with All Hallows, London Wall, form an arc around the perimeter of the City. For good measure add the church of St Katharine Creed, built in 1628-31, which also escaped the Fire and you can then complete your survey of non-Wren churches of London by including St Mary Woolnoth by Hawksmoor. There are still many places in the City where churches can be found and which offer much to the seeker of curiosities.

The churches are described in alphabetical order, but reference to the map will enable the curiosity hunter to visit them in the numbered order, though no doubt several trips will be necessary to complete the circuit.

Although better known today as **All-Hallows-by-the-Tower** (19) it also boasts of being 'All Hallows Barkingchurch'; the latter title reminds us that once this church was owned by the Abbey Church of Barking, a convent set up by St Erkenwald whose sister was Abbess. One of the few churches to survive the Great Fire, it was damaged again in the Second World War, when a Saxon doorway and part of a cross were exposed. In the crypt under the church can be seen a model of Roman Londinium, remains of a Roman villa, monumental brasses and coffin plates. As the church is on the edge of Tower Hill a number of those executed there were buried in the church. The body of Archbishop Laud, who was executed

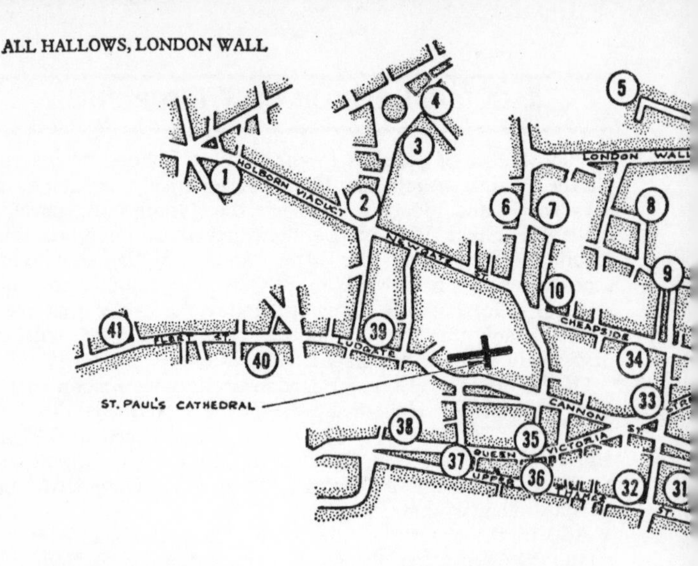

1. St Andrew, Holborn
2. St Sepulchre without Newgate
3. St Bartholomew the Less
4. St Bartholomew the Great
5. St Giles, Cripplegate
6. St Botolph, Aldersgate
7. St Anne and St Agnes
8. St Mary, Aldermanbury
9. St Lawrence Jewry
10. St Vedast, Foster Lane
11. St Margaret, Lothbury
12. All Hallows, London Wall
13. St Botolph, Bishopsgate
14. St Ethelburga
15. St Helen, Bishopsgate
16. St Andrew Undershaft
17. St Katharine Cree
18. St Botolph, Aldgate
19. All-Hallows-by-the-Tower
20. St Olave, Hart Street
21. St Margaret Pattens

in 1645, was later transferred to St John's College, Oxford. In the church can be seen the football and sword of Sidney Woodruffe VC, whose ancestors named a nearby street.

All Hallows, London Wall (12), now a Guild Church and the headquarters of the Council for the Care of Churches, stands over London Wall. When it was a parish church before the last war, the preacher left his stall in the choir, entered the vestry—built on an old bastion of the wall, then walked up a short flight of steps, through a doorway into the pulpit in the church. By doing so he had left London and returned to preach!

Appropriately the church of **St Andrew, Holborn** (1), now houses the mortal remains of Thomas Coram, who began the Foundling Hospital in Hatton Gardens for deserted children in 1741—it was later moved to a new site in

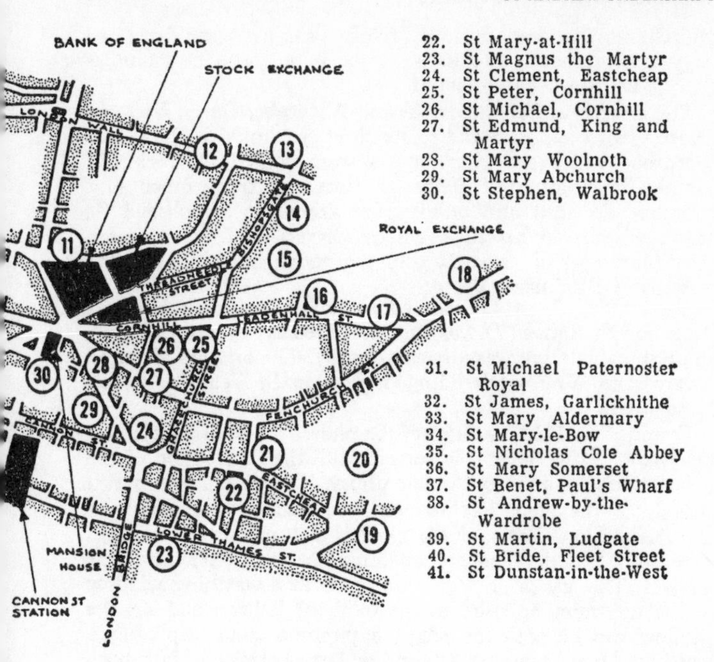

Lamb's Conduit Fields. The church is the headquarters of the London Diocesan Council for Youth. In addition, the pulpit, organ and font all come from the chapel of the Foundling Hospital. On the north wall of the church is a resurrection stone showing the world on doomsday when all the dead rise out of their graves and, after their souls have been duly weighed by St Michael the Archangel, some are allowed into the Heavenly City while others will be taken down to Hell. It is interesting to note that usually all are naked, except bishops and popes who come out of their coffins wearing their mitres and crowns.

One of the maypoles of the City was regularly erected in Leadenhall Street outside the church of **St Andrew Undershaft** (16), and after being used was strapped to the outside wall of the church—hence the suffix 'undershaft'. One of the greatest Londoners, John Stowe, whose famous book *A Survay of London* was first published in 1598, lies buried in the church, having died in 1605. Every year in April the Lord Mayor of London attends a service here and a new quill is placed in Stowe's right hand.

The church of **St Andrew-by-the-Wardrobe,** Queen Victoria Street (38), owes its suffix to its close proximity to the Great Wardrobe where the king's stores were housed. The church contains a number of items of furniture from other city churches. Its font and pulpit came from the demolished St Matthew's, Bread Street. From St Olave's, Old Jewry, came the Stuart coat of arms. Within the parish boundary are the remains of Blackfriars Priory.

Used today by a Latvian congregation, the church of **St Anne and St Agnes** (7) was once described as 'by-the-willows', so presumably there was a stream nearby. The original font and cover, from Wren's rebuilding, is now in St Vedast's, Foster Lane (10).

Founded in 1123 by Rahere, the church of **St Bartholomew the Great** (4) in Smithfield served, until the Dissolution of the Monasteries, as an Augustinian priory. Today it is the parish church of the area, having been acquired by the parish at the Dissolution. Parts of the church and monastic buildings were sold, the parishioners retaining the old choir for their services. The last prior, Prior Bolton, built a watching window in the triforium opposite to the tomb of Rahere, and on the window can be seen his rebus, a punning stone depicting a crossbow 'bolt' piercing a 'tun' or large barrel—a 'bolt-tun'. In the south aisle can be seen the memorial to Edward Cooke who died in 1652; the inscription asks the reader to cry for him, but if unable then 'yet stay and see the marble weep'. Made of weeping marble, in certain humid temperatures the stone does in fact appear to cry.

Founded at the same time as the hospital which it serves as its parish church, **St Bartholomew the Less** (3) has parts dating back to pre-Great Fire times: a fifteenth-century brass and some medieval carvings remain. The architect Inigo Jones (1573-1652) was baptised in the church; it was Jones who introduced Palladian architecture into the country after having visited buildings in Italy designed by Andrea Palladio.

Since 1877 **St Benet's, Paul's Wharf** (37), has been the Welsh Episcopalians' church where services are held in the Welsh language every Sunday. Inigo Jones was buried in the former church. At one time the galleries of the church were used by the College of Heralds. From a nearby wharf goods were unloaded for St Paul's Cathedral in the Middle Ages, hence the suffix 'Paul's Wharf'.

St Botolph's, Aldersgate (6), is one of three City churches dedicated to Botolph, the saint from Boston, Lincolnshire. It was rebuilt in the eighteenth century, possibly by Nathaniel Wright. The east window of eighteenth-century glass depicts the 'Agony in the Garden', the work of John Pearson from a painting by Nathaniel Clarkson. The memorial cloister erected at the instigation of G. F. Watts, the artist, commemorates everyday deeds of heroism. This church has now been made redundant and plans for its future include using it for a post office union museum or as a museum of church art.

St Botolph's, Aldgate (18), was rebuilt in 1725 by George Dance the elder (1692-1768), and has a ceiling designed by John Bentley, the architect of Westminster's Roman Catholic Cathedral, in the Art Nouveau style. When, in 1554, the Earl of Suffolk, Lady Jane Grey's father, was beheaded on Tower Hill his head was placed at Aldgate; it was later removed and buried in the forecourt of the church.

The parish church of **St Botolph's, Bishopsgate** (13), was rebuilt either by James Gold or by Giles Dance between 1725 and 1729. In the churchyard stands the former parish school, with its figure of a boy and girl in their uniform, which since 1952 has been the Hall of the Fanmakers Company.

A remarkable survivor of both the Great Fire and the Blitz is the Tudor lectern of **St Bride's Church**, Fleet Street (40). Before the restoration of the church in the 1950s extensive excavations were carried out by the Roman and Medieval London Excavation Council. The result can be seen in the crypt which displays buildings from Roman times (a tessellated pavement) to the charnel houses of the seventeenth century. The east wall of the church is, in fact, flat but has been cunningly painted, by Glyn Jones, to represent a round-ended apse.

Claiming to be the original 'Oranges and lemons' church of the nursery rhyme, **St Clement's, Eastcheap** (24), bases this statement on the fact that these fruits were once unloaded and sold within its boundaries. The church also has some bread shelves from which the charity bread was taken after the main service on Sunday. A number of churches in the City had money left to them from which they bought loaves of bread for distribution to the poor. In most instances today the moneys have either run out or have been incorporated in other charitable funds.

The present church of **St Dunstan-in-the-West** (41) dates

from 1832 when it was rebuilt by John Shaw, following the widening of Fleet Street. It is a copy of All Saints Church, The Pavement, York, and displays over the side entrance a contemporary statue of Queen Elizabeth I (1558-1603) which once stood over Ludgate but was removed here after the demolition of the gateway in the eighteenth century. The carved heads of John Donne, poet and Dean of St Paul's Cathedral (1572-1631), and Izaak Walton (1593-1683), author of *The Compleat Angler,* can be seen as arch stops over the main entrance to the church. Donne was vicar here from 1624 to 1625, and Walton lived in the parish and was a frequent worshipper at the church. The seventeenth-century clock from the former church has two sparsely clad attendants who club out the hours to wile away the time, and standing inside the doorway, under Elizabeth I, are the figures of King Lud and his sons.

Sir Christopher Wren's design for the spire of **St Edmund King and Martyr,** in Lombard Street (27), is shaped like a lighthouse, a reminder that after the Great Fire the nearby parish of St Nicholas, patron saint of seamen as well as children, merged with St Edmund's. Around the font cover once stood the twelve apostles, but now only four remain. This church was the only one damaged by bombing in the *First* World War.

Another medieval church in Bishopsgate is **St Ethelburga's** (14), named after the first abbess of Barking, the daughter of Ethelbert, the Christian king of Kent. The font, dating from the Middle Ages, has a Greek palindrome inscription of the nineteenth century. Sir Ninian Comper was responsible for the screen and loft, pews, pulpit, lectern and panelling.

One of the few remaining pre-Fire churches, **St Giles's, Cripplegate** (5), saw the marriage of Oliver Cromwell in 1620 to Elizabeth Bourchier and the burial of John Milton in 1674.

St Helen's Church (15) is in a secluded courtyard off Bishopsgate, surrounded by tall office buildings, and is, as formerly, a dual church, with half used by nuns in pre-Reformation times and half by the parish, with a wall down the centre to separate them. Dedicated to St Helen, the mother of the Emperor Constantine and discoverer of the True Cross, this is one of the real gems among the City's churches: in the north wall can be seen the squint or hagioscope through which the nuns in the infirmary beyond, or perhaps those being punished by not being allowed to attend mass, could see the altar. In the eastern portion of this side of the church are two tombs of interest: one is that of Sir Thomas Gresham, founder of the Royal Exchange, the other of Sir Julius Caesar. Also buried in the church, though the tomb is no longer above ground, was Bancroft, founder of Bancroft School at Woodford; following instructions in his will the sexton used regularly to visit his tomb and dust the coffin! Over the nuns' squint is the only Easter sepulchre left in the City, used to 'bury' the consecrated Host of the Mass on Maundy Thursday until, after due watch had been kept, it was resurrected on Easter Day. The fourteenth-century tomb of Sir John de Otesurich and his wife, from St Martin Outwhich's Chapel, demolished in 1874, are now in the south chapel of the church.

The original church of **St James, Garlickhithe** (32), was built in 1326, destroyed in 1666 and repaired after the Second World War. During restoration of the church in the nineteenth century a skeleton was found, but its identity nobody knows! Perhaps he was one of the six Lord Mayors buried here, or just an ordinary parishioner. It is said that the choir-boys used to dance him round the church, but now he is locked up in the vestibule cupboard.

At the dissolution of Holy Trinity Priory, Aldgate, Henry VIII offered the local people the great abbey church for worship, but they preferred the smaller church or chapel. Dedicated to **St Katharine** (17), with a curious suffix '**Cree**' which is a reminder of its original situation, Christ Church (Cree) being synonymous with Holy Trinity. Buried by the high altar is Sir John Gayer, Lord Mayor in 1646, who while on an expedition across an eastern desert became separated from his party and met a lion! He immediately fell on his knees and started praying, and when he opened his eyes the lion had moved away! In gratitude, he left money for a sermon to be preached on every anniversary. Although the money has now been absorbed into the general funds of the Parochial Charities of 1871, the sermon is still preached every October. In the south-west corner seek out the head (capital) belonging to a former church; if this is still in its original position, then the present church must be built on top!

Within the shadow of Guildhall—from where the City is governed—is the church of **St Lawrence Jewry** (9), with its curiously shaped weathervane showing a gridiron. Lawrence, martyred in A.D. 258, was burned alive over a gridiron, hence the sign; he is also the patron saint of the Girdlers' Company of London whose crest shows him with his gridiron. The beautiful modern stained-glass windows depict people closely associated with the former parish.

Once standing at the foot of the medieval London Bridge, the church of **St Magnus the Martyr,** Lower Thames Street (23), is now almost surrounded by office buildings. It was one of the first to be destroyed in the Great Fire and was rebuilt by Wren ten years later. Safely locked away in a reliquary is a relic of the True Cross which on every Good Friday is venerated by the faithful. Whether Miles Coverdale, translator of the first complete English Bible, would approve, is open to debate, as he preached against images and resigned his rectorship in 1563 for puritanical reasons. Originally buried in the church of St Bartholomew-by-the-Exchange (demolished in 1840) he was later translated here. In the churchyard are pieces of two former London Bridges, the medieval and the nineteenth-century bridges.

The suffix of **St Margaret, Lothbury** (11), comes either from the Lopa family who used to live here, or because it was a 'loathsome' place due to the proximity of the Founderers Company. At least three other churches designed by Wren have made their contribution to the beauty of this church. From All Hallows, Upper Thames Street, come the candelabra, the rood-screen—a match for that at St Peter's Cornhill in its rarity value—which was a gift of Theodore and Jacob Jacobsen in 1689, and the tester of the pulpit. St Olave Jewry provided the communion rail and the font, which is attributed to Grinling Gibbons. While from St Christopher-le-Stocks (demolished in 1781 to make room for an extension to the Bank of England) came the reredos.

Said by some to have obtained its strange suffix because pattens, a kind of shoe, were made in the parish, or because in medieval times a family called Patins were great benefactors of the church, today **St Margaret Pattens** church (21) provides an interesting oasis in the midst of an area full of offices. There are several unique features and items in the church: on the north side of the choir can be seen an ornately backed seat—this is the punishment seat, and here children who were misbehaving in church would be made to sit until the service was over. The beadle who brought the children to the chair had his own private pew behind it, and this too is worth examining for it is unique in the City. On the south wall of the church, in a glass-fronted cabinet, are samples of pattens, and buried nearby is James Donaldson, who was the City Garbler, an inspector of drugs in the seventeenth century. In the tower hangs a pre-Great Fire bell which can still be heard tolling over the City it has served so well. At the back of the church, and standing on either side of the entrance doorway are a set of raised pews on whose ceiling are the initials C W, said, according to one writer, to stand for Christopher Wren, being his favourite church! It also stands for Church Warden!

Built hard against the west wall of the City, **St Martin's Ludgate** (39) acts as a foil for the cathedral at the top of the hill, with its leaden spire silhouetted against the sky and holding its own against the massive dome of St Paul's. The font has a Greek palindrome—a word or phrase which reads the same both ways—on it. The translation reads 'Wash my sin, not my face only'.

Under the forecourt of **St Mary Abchurch** (29) is the medieval crypt of the church destroyed in the Fire, which was rediscovered after an air-raid during the last war. A letter, found in 1946, signed by Grinling Gibbons (1648-1721), confirms that he did much of the carving here.

As a memorial to Sir Winston Churchill, the former church of **St Mary, Aldermanbury** (8), was transferred bodily in 1966 to Westminster College, University of Fulton, Missouri, in the United States of America, where Sir Winston made his famous Iron Curtain speech in 1946. The site has now been laid out as a garden and the medieval walls exposed to view. During the excavation of the site the grave of Bloody Judge Jeffreys was rediscovered. Standing in the former churchyard is a memorial to Heminge and Condell, publishers of Shakespeare's plays in the early seventeenth century.

In Queen Victoria Street, **St Mary Aldermary** (elder Mary) church (33) displays Gothic architecture designed by Wren. Notice particularly the fan-vaulting.

Built on pre-Conquest arches ('bows') the church of **St Mary le Bow,** Cheapside (34), has an interior completely rebuilt since the blitz of 1940-41. The Hanging Rood (the Crucifixion of Christ with attendant figures of Saint Mary and Saint John) was a gift by the Church of Germany as an act of reparation; it was carved in Oberammergau. Children born within the sound of Bow bells are 'registered' as Cockneys. The balcony over the entrance doorway to the church was put there by Wren and was intended to be used by kings and queens watching tournaments and processions in Cheapside, but it has never been used. Although Charles II was to have watched a procession from it, he heard rumours of a possible assassination plot and stayed at home!

Damaged in the Great Fire, and later rebuilt by Wren, the church of **St Mary-at-Hill** (22), standing on rising ground that once led down to the Thames, was again severely damaged by fire in May 1988. Restoration work should be complete in 1990. Stowe records that Thomas Becket was rector here in the twelfth century. One of the three Hill organs in London is installed here (another is at St John's Church, Hyde Park Crescent).

All that is left of the church of **St Mary Somerset** (36) is the Wren tower, within which is a student's bed-sitting room. The remainder of the church was demolished in 1871.

The parish church of **St Mary Woolnoth** (28), designed by Nicholas Hawksmoor in the early eighteenth century, stands over the entrances of Bank underground station. Compensation of £250,000 was paid in 1901 when the station was extended. Notice how the architect, by excluding all windows in the lower storeys of the church, turns the building into an almost sound-proof box. Edward Lloyd, in whose coffee-house in Tower Street Lloyd's of London was founded in 1689, was buried in the church in 1713, his coffee-house having moved to Lombard Street some time before.

When Wren designed a new church for the parish of **St Michael, Cornhill** (26), after the Fire, he was given clear instructions that it should be in the Gothic style and not, as he would have doubtless preferred, in the new Renaissance form. In Saxon times the church was given to the Abbey of Evesham in Worcestershire who maintained connections with the parish until the Dissolution of the Monasteries. The tower is a facsimile of the chapel tower at Magdalen College, Oxford. Somewhere in the former churchyard, now laid out as a garden, lie buried the father and grandfather of John Stowe, the sixteenth-century historian and writer.

At the foot of College Hill stands Dick Whittington's church, **St Michael Paternoster Royal** (31), whose suffix reminds one that here is the Vintry Ward where in the Middle Ages wine was unloaded, particularly from La Reole near Bordeaux. The 'Paternoster' comes from a nearby Paternoster (Our Father) home where rosaries were made. A modern stained-glass window depicts Dick Whittington and his cat. In a restoration of the church a mummified cat was found in the roof of the building—was it Dick Whittington's?

Now no longer a parish church, **St Nicholas Cole Abbey** (35) is used by the Free Church of Scotland and is the ward church for Queenhithe. It houses a number of original carvings by Grinling

Gibbons which survived the fires of 1940. Its weathervane is a ship and reminds us that St Nicholas is the patron saint of sailors. The suffix 'Cole Abbey' may come from a medieval benefactor or, more likely, from the 'cold arbour' which stood nearby — a shelter for vagrants in days gone by.

With the site of the Navy Office across the roadway in Seething Lane, where could be a more natural burial place for Samuel Pepys, Secretary of the Navy Office in the seventeenth century, than **St Olave's Church,** Hart Street (20), renamed by Charles Dickens in his book the *Uncommercial Traveller* as ' Saint Ghastley Grim ' because of the archway with skulls forming part of the decoration. The skulls are a reminder that the churchyard was used in 1658 as a burial place for persons who died of a plague in that year. The church was one of the few to survive the Great Fire. St Benet's, Gracechurch Street (demolished 1867), provided the pulpit and St Katherine Colman supplied an organ keyboard whose white notes were black! The parish registers reveal that Mother Goose was buried here!

On the highest point of the City stands the church of **St Peter, Cornhill** (25)—as some would have us believe, on the site of the oldest church in London. The story has been told of how a certain King Lucius, himself a legendary figure, founded it as the principal church of his kingdom. This church is one of only two—the other being St Margaret Lothbury—to possess a post-Great Fire rood-screen. Originally these screens would have had the crucifixion scene on them to remind the faithful of Christ's death; today they simply divide the nave from the choir. Nearly all the woodwork of this church is original seventeenth-century and can easily be identified by its colour—blood red or brown. Wren gave instructions that all wood should be dipped in animals' blood in Smithfield Market before being stained. In the vestry can be seen a brass plaque commemorating the early foundation of the parish, and the original Father Smith keyboard belonging to the organ he built for the church, and on which Mendelssohn played in September 1840. However, the largest object in the room is a withdrawing table, which is unique; used in the church for communion services it was removed—withdrawn—after use, thereby emphasising the Protestant faith's belief that the service is not a sacrifice on an altar. Outside the vestry, high on the wall, are the former bread shelves. On the building to the right of the main entrance of the church, in Cornhill, can be seen the 'Unholy Trinity', three devils. Placed there by an architect who lost a dispute with the rector and churchwardens, they record his personal feelings towards the people of the church.

The present church of **St Sepulchre without Newgate** (2), on the site of a Saxon church, was rebuilt in 1440 by Sir John Popham, and although only damaged at the time of the Great Fire it was repaired by Wren. The exterior of the church shows many of the architectural features associated with the Gothic (medieval) form, including the windows reinstated in the nineteenth century, where the interior is all one would expect of Wren and the Renaissance. Being in close proximity to the Old Bailey, the Central Criminal Court, which stands on the site of Newgate Prison, it is not surprising that the church has many stories connected with them. Robert Dowe left a bequest of £50 in his will in order that on the eve of executions a man might exhort those about to die to repent. At midnight a bell would be rung outside the cell and a short verse recited for the 'benefit' of its inmates. The handbell can be seen in the church. Towards the end of the south wall of the church is a blocked archway which once led to a tunnel under the street outside, through which the verger would go to call the condemned men to repentance in Newgate Prison opposite. Also in the south aisle lies buried Captain John Smith (1580-1631), the cartographer and founder of Virginia in the American Colonies. A window nearby commemorates the young Red Indian princess who saved the life of Captain Smith and was brought to England by him to avoid possible reprisals by members of her tribe. The late Sir Henry Wood learnt to play the organ here, and in the Chapel of St Cecilia, the patron saint of music, is a window to his memory; his ashes are buried in the chapel.

Standing originally by the side of the river Walbrook—hence its suffix—the church of **St Stephen Walbrook** (30), can today be found nestling behind the Mansion House. The dome is reckoned by many an architectural historian to be the prototype for St Paul's Cathedral, and is certainly one of the finest by Wren. Sir John Vanbrugh was buried in the church in his family's vault. Today the church serves as a centre for the Samaritans and has been thoroughly restored, with an altar by the late Henry Moore.

Twelve former parishes are combined in the present parish of **St Vedast,** Foster Lane (10), the only church in London to bear this dedication. Indeed there is record of only two others in England, one at Norwich where now only a street bears his name and the other at Tathwell in Lincolnshire. Vedast was Bishop of Arras, in France, in the sixth century. During the restoration of the 1960s several items of furniture from other Wren churches were brought here: the font from St Anne and St Agnes (7); the pulpit from All Hallows, Bread Street (demolished 1878); the carved organ case from St Bartholomew-by-Exchange; while the reredos was designed for St Christopher-le-Stocks, which was pulled down in 1781. The ceiling of the church is painted with silver, aluminium and gilt.

6. INNS AND THEIR CURIOSITIES

The original definition of an 'inn' was a place where food, drink and lodgings could be obtained, whereas a 'tavern', strictly speaking, only sold drink, and woe betide the landlords of either who broke the law. Fitzstephen, writing in the twelfth century, said that London had two plagues, 'fire and drink', the former being inevitable, considering that most buildings were made of wood, and the latter being an accepted fact. He also tells of how young men 'in their cups' would ring the bells of the local churches. Considering the number of churches at that time this must have caused quite a noise. The keynote of the medieval inn was simplicity, with dormitory bedrooms shared by both sexes; a bowl of soup cost a farthing, the bed a halfpenny, a candle a farthing.

Hidden among the nineteenth-century warehouses and half obscured by a railway bridge, at Bankside is the **Anchor** (6). Shakespeare came here, perhaps between acts from the nearby Globe Theatre, and later Dr Johnson, who obviously found compiling a dictionary of the English language very thirsty work. You may hear stories of the river pirates selling their ill-gotten gains to the barman; there are tales too, of escapes from the Clink Prison across the street, and of how it was a favourite hunting spot for members of the press gang, whose job was to impress upon the fit and hearty man the need to join the Navy.

There can be little doubt that rebuilding a city is thirsty work. The **Bell** (14), with entrances in Fleet Street and Brides Lane, was quickly rebuilt after the Fire to help sustain Wren's workmen.

The story of the Blackfriars is told elsewhere in this book

(page 23) but their lasting memorial today is the **Black Friar** public house at the end of Queen Victoria Street (19). Built originally in the early seventeenth century and rebuilt in 1903, it was decorated by Henry Poole RA in the Art Nouveau style, depicting in marble, bronze, wood and glass the everyday happenings of the monastery; but do not miss the direction signs outside pointing the way to the saloon bar.

George IV was once attending a cock-fight in the vicinity of the **Castle** inn, Cowcross Street (13), when he ran out of cash. Although the landlord did not recognise him, after a slight argument he loaned him thirty shillings on the king's father's watch. After having won the bet for which he needed the money, George IV thought of having the landlord knighted but, because he had failed to recognise the king, he gave the 'house' a pawnbrokers' licence in perpetuity instead. The three brass balls are still in the bar, but whether you can 'hock' anything remains to be seen.

Perhaps the most famous pub in all Britain is the **Cheshire Cheese,** Fleet Street (15); visitors from all over the world place it high on their list. One of the Fleet Street 'homes' of Dr Samuel Johnson, it has also attracted many literary giants in its time. There is a story told of a great fan of the Doctor who on receiving his soup asked if it could be served in a dish used by Samuel Johnson. Doubtless with an eye to a possible tip, the waiter went away and found the most chipped dish on the premises and served the soup in it. The Cheshire Cheese was also noted for its parrot, whose vocabulary of 'blue' language was surpassed by none, and connoisseurs from far and wide would come to listen to the bird. When it caught cold and died, its death was solemnly announced by the BBC and reported in newspapers all over the world, including the *North China Star.*

You can almost hear the cocks crowing at the **Cockpit** in St Andrew's Hill (11), for the interior shows what a cockpit looked like, while the pictures on the walls show many a proud old cock strutting about in triumph. The inn sign incorporates a pair of dice, and the cockpit gallery is still there although not accessible to members of the public.

The **Crutched Friar** in Crosswall Street (20) is so called because near to this street stood a monastic house whose friars wore a large leather cross as part of their habit—hence the crossed or crutched friars.

A 'left-at-the-church' gentleman of the eighteenth century, named either Nicholas or Nathaniel Bentley, sealed up the

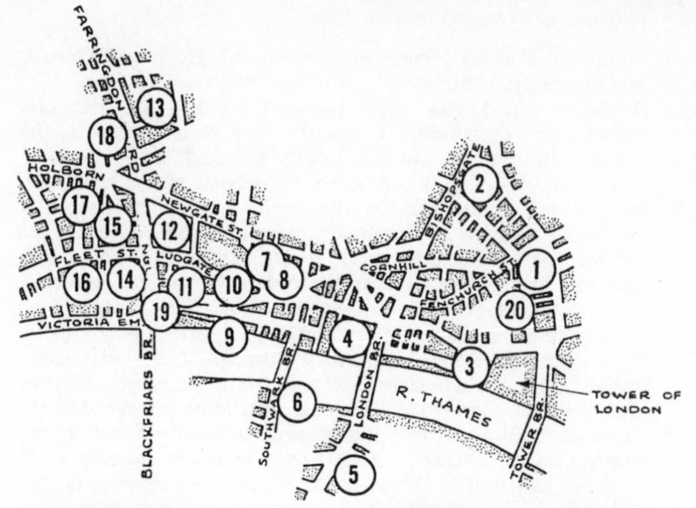

1. Hoop and Grapes, Aldgate High Street
2. **Dirty Dick's, Bishopsgate**
3. **Tiger Tavern, Tower Hill**
4. **Old Wine Shades, Martin Lane**
5. **George, Borough High Street**
6. **Anchor, Bankside**
7. **Williamson's, Bow Lane**
8. **Ye Olde Watling, Watling Street**
9. **Samuel Pepys, off Upper Thames Street**
10. **Horn, Knightrider Street**
11. **Cockpit, St Andrew's Hill**
12. **Rumboe Tavern, Old Bailey**
13. **Castle, Cowcross Street**
14. **Bell, Fleet Street/Bride's Lane**
15. **Cheshire Cheese, Fleet Street**
16. **Olde Cock Tavern, Fleet Street**
17. **Printer's Devil, New Fetter Lane**
18. **Mitre, Ely Court, off Hatton Gardens**
19. **Black Friar, Queen Victoria Street**
20. **Crutched Friar, Crosswall Street**

room in which his wedding breakfast was to have taken place and became a ragged eccentric instead. A far-seeing landlord of a tavern in Bishopsgate, **Dirty Dick's** (2), bought the room and turned it into a bar and today it attracts many tourists.

When Shakespeare was not imbibing at the Anchor on bankside he would be found at the **George,** in the Borough High Street (5) which is the only galleried inn left in London. Owned today by the National Trust, and therefore a protected building in the fullest sense of the word, it is only a shadow of its former self, as earlier in this century the other three sides of the inn-yard were pulled down to make way for a larger unloading bay for the railway company. In order to get to the upper rooms one still has to use the original outside staircase.

Scheduled as an ancient monument, the **Hoop and Grapes,** in Aldgate High Street (1), is one of the few pre-Great Fire buildings still in use. The previous building on the site, dating from the thirteenth century, was rebuilt early in the seventeenth century, but the cellars are said to be those of the original building. Long before the advent of the telephone, the means of communication with the kitchen staff was through the wall—through a 'lug-hole'; this curiously shaped hole allowed the landlord to speak to the staff, who would put their ear to the hole to hear the orders for meals. However, in more recent years this device has fallen into disuse.

The present building of the **Horn,** Knightrider Street (10), dates from the eighteenth century although it was first mentioned in 1687 when several officers from the nearby College of Arms met there to discuss the rebuilding of the college. There is still a distinct Dickensian atmosphere about the house, Charles Dickens's bust smiles benignly from a shelf over the bar, and it is not hard to imagine members of the Pickwick Club frequenting the place in order to buy wine for the unlucky Mr Pickwick languishing in the Fleet Prison as a result of Mrs Bardell's breach of promise suit. While the area was being redeveloped in the 1980s the inn was completely restored down to the last detail of the original.

The foundation date on the stone on the outside of the **Mitre,** Mitre Place (18)—off Hatton Gardens and leading to Ely Place—is given as 1547. But being so near to the Bishop of Ely's town house there could have been an inn on this corner long before that time. Inside, propping up one corner of the building is a cherry-tree trunk around which Queen Elizabeth I is said to have danced, perhaps with her favourite of the time, Sir Christopher Hatton, joining in. For a time the tavern observed Cambridgeshire licensing hours, which was very convenient when they did not agree with the rest of London.

Although it moved to the other side of the street in the nineteenth century, the **Olde Cock Tavern** in Fleet Street (16) is still worth a visit to hear the tales of Pepys who was a frequenter of the previous house, or to see the original inn sign carved by Grinling Gibbons.

Built over three hundred years ago, surviving both the Great Fire and the Blitz, the **Old Wine Shades** (4) in Martin Lane, off Cannon Street, only a stone's throw from where the Fire started, provides a quiet oasis in which to partake of your favourite sherry or wine. Dickens, we are told, was a frequent visitor here and enjoyed its old-world atmosphere as much as do visitors today.

In 1957, presumably because there were more printers than vintners in the region of Fetter Lane, the brewery renamed their pub from the Vintner's to the **Printer's Devil** (17). Named after a young boy, imp or devil, who did all the odd jobs about the printer's workshop the pub houses a museum of the history of prints and printing on its walls. In addition to photographs, prints and other samples of a printer's work there are also two working models of printing presses of the nineteenth century.

In Hillgate House, Old Bailey, is the **Rumboe Tavern** (12) and being so near to the site of Newgate Prison it is hardly surprising that the decor is on the subject of prison and prisoners.

Housed in an old warehouse, close to Queenhithe, overlooking the river is the **Samuel Pepys** (9). Part of the decoration around the walls consists of extracts from the famous Diary of Pepys. From the pub's balconies one can watch the sun set over London, or the river pass by.

Rebuilt in the 1960s the **Tiger Tavern,** Tower Hill (3), has a history that could well fill a book on its own. In the upper bar a mummified cat can be seen, by pressing a light switch on the wall, said to have been stroked by Elizabeth I. While she was imprisoned in the Tower of London by her father and later by her sister, she managed to escape from the dreary life of a prisoner by using an underground tunnel, said still to exist, and to have enjoyed a quiet drink or two in the Tiger Tavern before returning to the Tower. An interesting ceremony takes place here every 10 years when the beer is tested. The Lord Mayor of London and his retinue, bringing with them their own personal beer-taster, are duly received by mine host; the beer-taster, wearing leather breeches, sits on a stool on to which a sample of the beer has been poured—if he sticks to the stool then the beer is good, and then all enjoy drinks on the house. The landlord has a garland placed round his neck and a laurel leaf bouquet is hung outside the door. The test has never been known to fail.

In Groveland Court, a cul-de-sac alley off Bow Lane, is **Williamsons Tavern** (7) which dates back to the eighteenth century when a Mr Williamson turned the house into a tavern or inn. Built on the site of the home of Sir John Falstaff it had a large banqueting hall, said, by some, to be the original Mansion House, where a seventeenth-century Lord Mayor entertained William and Mary to dinner. Before dining, the royal guests presented the Lord Mayor with a pair of wrought-iron gates, which he accepted, but ordered them to be taken outside. The Queen, angry at this, had them brought back again! Today they form the end of the alley. The Mansion House story is perpetuated by a room called The Mansion House Lounge. Also inside the house is an inscribed stone stating that it stands in the 'centre of London'. Evidence of an even earlier house on the site was discovered during the rebuilding after the last war, when Roman tiles were found—they now form part of a fireplace.

Old photographs taken in the early part of this century show **Ye Olde Watling** as a restaurant (8). Its original licence stated that a meal had to be ordered before a drink could be allowed. Today the tavern is a pleasant oasis surrounded by the offices and shops of a very busy City.

INDEX